End

Have you ever given any thought to the moment you will leave this earth and find yourself on the streets of gold? Have you tried to imagine the joyful faces awaiting your arrival? Seeing Jesus for the very first time face to face? Priceless! Mothers, fathers, brothers, sisters, grandparents, children, friends—it seems surreal. Maybe we'll find ourselves surrounded by that great cloud of witnesses or perhaps the people whose lives we may have influenced in some way over our lifetime. That "Welcome Home Children" moment will be hard to beat!

Scripture tells that "eye hath not seen, nor ear heard, neither have entered into the heart of man, the things which God hath prepared for them that love Him." Certainly, a great adventure awaits—far better than any dreams and conversations we might have! Who can possibly wrap their arms around spending eternity with the Creator of the Universe? And don't we all long to hear the words, "Well done thou good and faithful servant?"

Recently I watched an interview with an aging rock star from the 70s who acknowledged his absolute terror at the thought of dying. Yet no thought was given to living forever in the presence of the King. It never entered his mind. Sadly, in this age of biblical illiteracy, many Christians share his fear, terrified of their future. They cling to this world with unbridled passion, seeking whatever limited joy one can have on earth, delaying the inevitable. Yet the greatest moment in the life of a believer, the rapture and our imminent arrival in heaven, should be our greatest triumph! I'm free! Free at last!

Free from sin, from pain and from death, never to be separated from Jesus and our families ever again! Be encouraged! He's coming for us soon.

This is where my dear friend's book shines. Pastor Larry, if you've never met him, is a great encourager. It was obvious from the very first day we met that he was not part of the "what's in it for me" crowd. His wisdom is freely offered to others and his knowledge of God's Word is second to none. Finally, you will understand that there is a backstory, a prequel if you will, to God's Creation and our need for a Savior. *A Place Called Heaven* will take you places you have never been before and then take you to the place we all desire. Once you finish this gem, you'll understand the Bible like never before. And you will have a longing deep in your soul for meeting Jesus—without any fear!

BOB ULRICH
Prophecy Watchers
Co-Founder

Have you ever truly contemplated heaven? What will it be like? What will we be like? With all the vast beauty and creation we see on the earth, can we even begin to envision the magnificent glory that awaits us as believers? The Bible is chock-full of promises to which we often say, "yes and amen," but when it comes to eternity and heaven, are the Scriptures too grand to understand?

Dr. Larry Ollison has given us great counsel on life's difficulties in several of his previous books by bringing simple steps to the practicality of living out God's Word victoriously here on earth. In *A Place Called Heaven*, Dr. Ollison once again brings clarity to Scripture, unraveling some of the mystery and reminding us of the promises of the Almighty God to His redeemed.

As is his gift, Dr. Ollison prompts us to investigate what can otherwise be a complex and weighty subject with a fresh look at the simplicity of Scripture. He invites us to meditate on the goodness of God for those who love Him, and even more, to accept the truth of how those Scriptures apply to each of us as heirs of God and joint-heirs with Jesus! Allow that to sink in. Are you a joint-heir with Jesus?

As he has done so well before, Dr. Ollison brings us into better understanding so we can fully live in the assurance of the hope that we have through Jesus Christ. In *A Place Called Heaven*, he brings familiar Bible passages right off the page and helps us grasp the fullness of God's promises to us, not just here on earth, but in eternity.

Enjoy and explore—you'll be encouraged!

TAMARA SCOTT
Host, *Truth for Our Time*

Dr. Larry Ollison's newest book, *A Place Called Heaven*, is truly a masterpiece! Dr. Ollison has gathered the most sought-after answers to the most age-old questions about heaven and the revelations from God's Word that present clear and understandable information about our future home.

With his deep understanding of the Hebrew language and culture, Larry settles once and for all many of the entangled perspectives about this amazing place.

I am especially grateful for his insight into the musical realities of our eternal destination and the vital importance of our music here on the earth flowing with the divine frequencies of this very real and totally alive place. "On earth as it is in heaven" takes on its fullest significance as we rehearse for our grand entrance!

I'm so thankful to God that He has moved through Dr. Ollison to bring to us this accurate, balanced and truly vibrant work of the Holy Spirit. Finally, a concise and understandable literary work on our eternal home!

LEN MINK
Len Mink Ministries

What happens when we die? Can we really believe in the hope that is written in the pages of our Bibles about a life after death? Is there a supernatural world that is more real than the one we find ourselves in?

Pastor Larry Ollison takes us on a wonderful journey through the pages of Scripture and opens the door to the reality of the heavenly realms. Some of the testimonies and stories found in these pages bolster our faith and give us deep insight into the heavenly world that awaits those of us who have come to know our Savior, Jesus, the soon-to-return King!

DR. L. A. MARZULLI
Spiral of Life Ministries
Author, Filmmaker

A Place Called

HEAVEN

YOUR JOURNEY HOME

HARRISON HOUSE BOOKS BY LARRY OLLISON

The Paradise of God

Finding Hope When Things Look Hopeless

Unlocking the Mysteries of the Holy Spirit

Life is in the Blood

Breaking the Cycle of Offense

The Practical Handbook for Christian Living

The Power of Grace

DR. LARRY OLLISON

A Place Called

HEAVEN

YOUR JOURNEY HOME

Published by Harrison House Publishers
Shippensburg, PA 17257

Cover design by Sarah Loehr
Interior design by Terry Clifton

ISBN 13 TP: 978-1-6803-1497-7
ISBN 13 eBook: 978-1-6803-1498-4
ISBN 13 HC: 978-1-6803-1500-4
ISBN 13 LP: 978-1-6803-1499-1

For Worldwide Distribution, Printed in the U.S.A.
1 2 3 4 5 6 7 8 / 24 23 22 21 20

CONTENTS

FOREWORD

Without reservation, I endorse this book on the believer's heavenly home by Dr. Larry Ollison. He and I have enjoyed much discourse on the "end of days" events and the prophetic future of the Church, which is Christ's body.

For me personally, it is a particularly rare joy to speak of these holy and wondrous things with someone who studies and understands them to such a degree.

Earth is not our home. We are pilgrims and sojourners here. You will be blessed and illuminated as you savor the journey to heaven and the glory of the heavenly Jerusalem, the eternal home of the Bride of Christ.

Dr. Billye Brim
Billye Brim Ministries

FOREWORD

Untold thousands of Christians have pondered Christ's words, when at the beginning of the fourteenth chapter of John, He said, "I go to prepare a place for you. And if I go and prepare a place for you, I will come again, and receive you unto myself; that where I am, there ye may be also." This simple statement has brought forth an almost endless number of questions about the "what, where, when, and why" of His miraculous promise. Larry Ollison devoutly believes and wonderfully explains this and many other Scriptural promises about heaven and eternity.

His years of study have taken him to a level of faith and understanding that makes it an effortless pleasure for him to describe our future and eternal place of residence. To the saints, Christ's promise is certainly one of the most amazing statements in human history.

This book is dedicated to making that "place" in heaven a comforting reality. After all, Christians have looked toward it as their "blessed hope" for centuries. Heaven can sometimes be viewed as an abstraction, or an idea that seems distant and uncertain. But within the setting of Larry's lifetime of work and teaching comes the deeper meaning of Christ's message. He's a great example of those among us whose lives bring encouragement to others—perhaps his greatest gifting.

His long experience in ministry has given him a special kind of wisdom that results in an ability to deal with unanswered questions. If you're around him for long, you'll notice this ability to comfort the saints.

I've seen Larry face challenges and frustrations, and I can say without a doubt that his faith is real. Likewise, the path of his life has brought him a special wisdom to anticipate common human experience, and to counsel effectively. You'll be encouraged by the observations about heaven that he delivers in a "down-to-earth" fashion.

GARY STEARMAN
Prophecy Watchers

INTRODUCTION

*In My Father's house are many mansions; if it were
not so, I would have told you. I go to prepare a place
for you. And if I go and prepare a place for you, I will
come again and receive you to Myself; that where I am,
there you may be also.*

JOHN 14:2-3

Heaven is a real place. Throughout the centuries there have
been novels and theater productions that have portrayed fictional characterizations of heaven, but heaven is not a fictional
place. Within the sixty-six books of the Holy Scriptures, we
are given intricate detail of the creation, location, and purpose
of heaven. We are told of past, present, and future events in
this glorious place called heaven.

Within the heavens there is currently a heavenly city and we are told of its magnificent future renovation. The Bible gives us great detail of this heavenly city as it is now and as it will be. It is the future home for the saints of God.

The Church age lies between two events. It began when Jesus placed His blood on the altar in heaven on the day of His resurrection. The Church age will end when He returns to "catch away" His Church to be His bride.

Several years after the ascension of Jesus (during the Church age), the Apostle Paul visited heaven. Since that time, many other believers have had heavenly visions, dreams, and encounters. Paul became a Christian by receiving Jesus as his Lord the same way people today receive Jesus as Lord. Anything Paul experienced as a first-century Christian is available to last-century Christians. If it happened to Paul, it is possible for it to happen to you because we are still in the Church age. While we will share some contemporary accounts of heavenly encounters, the standard for truth must always be the Holy Scriptures.

The main goal of this book is to reveal to the believer the glorious transition that takes place when they depart from this physical life into their life in heaven. Hidden throughout the Scriptures are precious golden nuggets of truth that reveal what our future heavenly home will be like.

First Corinthians 2:9 tells us that our earthly eyes have not seen, our earthly ears have not heard, and the natural hearts of men cannot comprehend what God has prepared for those who love Him. But the next verse tells us that the Holy Spirit has revealed these secret things to us, even the deep things to come.

So, if someone tells you that it's impossible to know what the place Jesus is preparing for us will be like, you will know the truth. He has revealed it through His Word by the revelation of the Holy Spirit.

As we journey together through the pages of this book, I encourage you to allow the Spirit of Truth to excite you and to build great anticipation within you for your future. Your best days are yet to come!

Chapter One

WHAT HAPPENS WHEN YOU DIE

Beloved brothers and sisters, we want you to be quite certain about the truth concerning those who have passed away, so that you won't be overwhelmed with grief like many others who have no hope.

1 THESSALONIANS 4:13 (TPT)

A few months ago, I officiated my younger sister's funeral; we were very close, so for her to depart to heaven has, of course, left an empty place in my heart. When her children asked me to officiate the funeral, my first thought was, "I will never be able to do that." But after prayer, I decided that since they asked, I would accept. The funeral was held at Bethel Mennonite Church, in the middle of farmland Missouri. Driving through the countryside to the church, it was not uncommon to see horse-drawn buggies like in the movies. It was a very picturesque scene.

As the funeral service began, another minister stood to read the obituary. Next, the song "You Raise Me Up" by Josh Groban was to play. Then I would stand at the pulpit of the small Mennonite church to give the eulogy for my sister. She loved to listen to that song; her daughter told me that in her final weeks, she had listened to it continually. I could feel my throat tightening as the obituary concluded and the song was ready to start. Then God came through once again and gave me strength in time of trouble. The sound man played the wrong track.

In that little country Mennonite church, instead of "You Raise Me Up," he played very loudly and boldly, "Sittin' on the Dock of the Bay" by Otis Redding. I'm quite sure this 150-year-old church—which was crafted from wood shipped in from Holland—that had horses and buggies outside and bonnets on the ladies inside, never had Otis Redding perform within its hallowed walls before! The somber mood lightened up and with great respect and joy, my sister was honored through the eulogy. The service concluded with the song, "You Raise Me Up," and I realized once again, no matter how good our plans are, God always has a better plan!

That day God reminded me of the truth in His Word and the promise that He has given to us who believe. I realized that everyone in my family was at my sister's funeral except for one family member: my sister. When she took her last breath, she departed. Although it is used as a cliché so many times, she actually *was* in a better place, free from the pain and the restrictions of her physical body.

I remember standing in the cemetery next to the little church as they placed my sister's casket into the ground. Unlike in the city, there were green fields as far as I could see in any direction. There was no freeway nearby, no sound of traffic, no airplanes overhead, just the silence that comes from being alone with God. As I recalled the closing song, I felt the Spirit of God speak quietly in my heart and say, "I will raise her up."

People tried their best to speak comforting words to members of the family. I remember someone saying, "I'm sorry you lost your sister." I knew what they meant, and I appreciated the kind remark, but deep inside I knew that my sister wasn't lost. I knew very well where she was, and according to Scripture, she knew where she was. Although there will always be a vacancy in my heart while I'm on this side of heaven, I have the assurance that what God has promised will come to pass. There will be a day when she and I will be together again and talk about what we'll do for the next million years or so. It will be a glorious day!

Questions About Life After Death

Through the years, I have discovered that most people do not have an understanding of what happens to their loved one when their physical body dies. Questions linger in their minds. Is there really life after death? Did they cease to exist? Are they in some type of suspended animation or soul sleep? Are they in heaven or hell? Can they experience anything without their body? Do they have memories, desires, and an understanding of their future?

Because of written fiction and Hollywood movies about heaven—as well as some ministers teaching it incorrectly—a lot of people are confused. Sometimes they leave the funeral with even more questions. This should not be! Why? Because the Bible clearly gives answers to these questions, and more. You don't have to be a Bible scholar to understand life after death. You just need to know and believe what the Bible says.

As a minister, I have been with many people when they took their last breath. At that moment, the human body begins to return to the dust from which God created it. Although we use the phrase "the person has died," we must never forget that human beings are spirits, possessing a soul, and living in a physical body (1 Thessalonians 5:23). The body is merely the container we live in, and when that container is destroyed, we depart to one of two places.

According to the Bible, in this current dispensation of grace, we are escorted by angels (Luke 16:22) to Paradise in heaven (2 Corinthians 12:2-4), or we are sent to Hades (Revelation 20:13), which is sometimes referred to as hell. Hades is the temporary holding place for the unrighteous dead where they will remain until the great white throne judgment, which will take place at the end of the millennial reign of Christ (Revelation

20:11-15). Regardless of which place you are taken to your spirit body will have certain attributes.

Spirit Bodies

Although we will discuss this further in the next chapter, you must know that during the time of the Old Covenant, and until the time Jesus ascended after His resurrection, there were two compartments in the heart of the earth: the bosom of Abraham (Paradise) and Hades. Jesus prophesied to His disciples that He would spend three days and three nights in the heart of the earth (Matthew 12:40); this was accomplished during the three days after His crucifixion.

In Luke chapter 16, Jesus tells a story that explains that riches—or lack of riches—do not determine our final destination. This event describes two actual people who lived and died on the earth. While the main purpose of the story was to show that earthly riches do not determine our entrance into the Kingdom of God, there are several subtle nuggets of truth that describe many attributes of a spirit body and reveal what happens after the physical body dies. Remember, this account occurred under the Old Covenant, when the bosom of Abraham (Paradise) was in the heart of the earth. Under the New Covenant, we find Paradise in heaven.

There was a certain rich man who was clothed in purple and fine linen and fared sumptuously every day. But there was a certain beggar named Lazarus, full of sores, who was laid at his gate, desiring to be fed with the crumbs which fell from the rich man's table. Moreover, the dogs came and licked his sores. So it was that the beggar died and was carried by the angels to Abraham's bosom. The rich man also died and was buried. And being in torments in Hades, he lifted up his eyes and saw Abraham afar off, and Lazarus in his bosom.

Then he cried and said, "Father Abraham, have mercy on me, and send Lazarus that he may dip the tip of his finger in water and cool my tongue, for I am tormented in this flame." But Abraham said, "Son, remember that in your lifetime you received your good things, and likewise, Lazarus evil things; but now he is comforted and you are tormented. And besides all this, between us and you there is a great gulf fixed, so that those who want to pass from here to you cannot, nor can those from there pass to us."

Then he said, "I beg you therefore, father, that you would send him to my father's house, for I have five brothers, that he may testify to them, lest they also come to this place of torment." Abraham said to him, "They have Moses and the prophets; let them hear them." And he said, "No, Father Abraham; but if one goes to them from the dead, they will repent." But he said to him, "If they do not hear Moses and the prophets, neither will they be persuaded though one rise from the dead."

Luke 16:19-31

This passage reveals a great number of things about Hades and the bosom of Abraham (Paradise), but what I would like to focus on here are the details concerning the bodies that these two individuals had after the death of their physical being.

Even though they did not have flesh and blood, nervous systems, and digestive systems, they still had attributes that were similar to those experienced by an earthly human being. Although they ended up in two different places in the heart of the earth, their spirits were still human spirits that possessed a type of spirit body.

These bodies were contained in such a way that they only inhabited certain places. They did not become omnipresent but were restricted to certain areas. Lazarus was escorted to a place of peace while the rich man was sent to Hades. Remember, Jesus was telling of this account before His resurrection, with Hades and the bosom of Abraham both being in the heart of the earth at that time, and there was a great gulf between them. The rich man could not leave Hades and Lazarus could not leave the bosom of Abraham.

Even without a physical body, there was the ability to suffer pain and torment. We know that sight can be experienced in a spirit body because the rich man could see Lazarus off in the distance. In their spirit bodies they could see, hear, and speak; they could carry on a conversation, even across the gulf between them. There was regret and desire in Hades and peace and comfort in the bosom of Abraham. There was a lack of water in Hades but an abundance in the bosom of Abraham. While this may not have been H_2O as we know it, it was a liquid substance that gave refreshing, and the unrighteous man couldn't get it. The unrighteous man even had the ability to bargain with Abraham, but he was told that the time of bargaining had passed.

We can see from this story that even without the physical body, our spirit man is very much alive and active with full sensory perceptions, desires, and abilities.

During this current dispensation of time (before the rapture of the Church), when a Christian dies, their physical flesh-and-blood body stays on the earth while their spirit is escorted by angels to Paradise in the third heaven. There they have full use of their faculties, completely experiencing the overwhelming joy of knowing they are with the Lord for eternity.

A Different Type of Sorrow

Paul wrote to the Thessalonian church:

> But I do not want you to be ignorant, brethren, concerning those who have fallen asleep, lest you sorrow as others who have no hope. For if we believe that Jesus died and rose again, even so God will bring with Him those who sleep in Jesus.
>
> For this we say to you by the word of the Lord, that we who are alive and remain until the coming of the Lord

will by no means precede those who are asleep. For the Lord Himself will descend from heaven with a shout, with the voice of an archangel, and with the trumpet of God. And the dead in Christ will rise first. Then we who are alive and remain shall be caught up together with them in the clouds to meet the Lord in the air. And thus, we shall always be with the Lord. Therefore comfort one another with these words.

1 THESSALONIANS 4:13-18

Putting all of this in context is important, so let's take a look at why Paul wrote this letter to the church in Thessalonica.

He wrote the letter around 50-51 AD. This was about twenty years after Jesus had ascended into heaven. Jesus told His followers He was leaving to prepare a place for them and He would return so they could be with Him eternally (John 14:2-3). This was great news for the young Church. Their Lord and Savior, the Creator of the universe, who came in the form of a man and rose from the dead, was coming back to get them after He had prepared a place for them somewhere in the heavens.

But as the years passed, some Christians died, and this young Church was asking Paul questions. Paul was an apostle and representative of Jesus on the earth to these young churches which were scattered throughout the known world. They asked, "What about the Christians who die before Jesus returns? Are they included in the glorious life to come in heaven for those who believe?" These were valid questions which Paul addressed completely in his letter.

Paul started his reply by telling them that he did not want them to be ignorant concerning their friends and families who were believers and had died (fallen asleep). He did not want them to be ignorant so they would not sorrow as the unbelievers sorrowed when their loved ones died. Paul said that knowing the truth about the believers who have fallen asleep would not eliminate sorrow, but it would be a different type of sorrow than the world has.

The word "ignorant" comes from the root word "ignore." If we ignore a subject, we become ignorant on that subject. Paul explicitly stated that as followers of Jesus, those young Christians should not ignore the subject of what happens when someone dies.

As Christians, we don't sorrow like the world sorrows. The world has no hope. Without Jesus, death brings finality and a forever separation from God. Without Jesus, death eliminates all hope of a future reconciliation with loved ones. Without Jesus, there is no hope. But Paul said we are not like the world who has no hope. Yes, we have a type of sorrow because the person who has passed away will be missed, and yes, there can be an emptiness in our life that this person once filled. But as a believer, Paul said our sorrow is tempered with joy because our relationship with the person who has passed is not over, but only put on hold.

A few years ago, my wife visited a close girlfriend that had moved to Australia, and she stayed almost a month. While she was gone, she was greatly missed. But as each day passed, I knew it was one day closer to her return. As time went by, the sorrow of her being gone was replaced by the joy of knowing she would return.

As Christians, we can experience the same joy when someone we love departs to Paradise. Although we miss them, knowing that we will see them again can soften the pain of the separation and bring great comfort and joy.

I'm sure almost everyone reading this has had a close friend or family member that has moved to heaven. These departed saints were loved, but as Christians, we have the knowledge and understanding that even though they have passed, they are still functioning and experiencing the joys of their new life. We also have comfort in knowing that they know they will see us again very soon. And even more so than we who remain, they know the truth of the Word that says, "For what is your life? It is even a vapor that appears for a little time and then vanishes away" (James 4:14). Of course, we know that is true because the Word says so, but they know it is true because they have experienced the shortness of life on earth in a physical body.

Although Paul's letter to the Thessalonians continues with more detail about the coming of the Lord, this portion of his letter closes with one of the most powerful, prophetic statements in the New Testament. He said that after the rapture of the Church, we will always be with the Lord, and know-ing that would bring great comfort (1 Thessalonians 4:17-18). In this one statement, he answers so many questions that are asked when a loved one dies. In this one statement, he reveals our eternal destiny.

So, where will we be in a thousand, million, billion, or trillion years? That question can be answered with this one statement: We will always be with the Lord. Throughout the tribulation, the millennium, and eternity we will be forever in close proximity to Jesus.

In the Cloud of Witnesses

When the last breath is taken, when the last heartbeat is com-plete, when the eyes see their last image in the physical realm, the spiritual eyes are opened, and the beautiful existence of God's kingdom begins to be realized. It is not uncommon for the spiritual eyes to open before the physical body quits work-ing. There are countless testimonies of people seeing loved ones and the glories of heaven as they transition into the eter-nal world. The spirit body continues when the physical body dies. As we drop off this earthly clothing, angels are standing by in their magnificence to escort us into the place the Lord has created for us.

Paradise is not our final destination, but it is a glorious place to be. It is an eternal place that will be our temporary residence while we wait to return with the Lord to meet the rest of the Body of Christ in the air and be reunited with our earthly bodies.

The Apostle Paul could not find words to describe this place when he was caught up into this heavenly realm (2 Corinthians 12:2-4), but the Bible tells us that it's a place of comfort. Because we will be interacting with the Lord, there will be great joy. Simply being in His presence brings fullness of joy (Psalm 16:11).

When we arrive, we automatically become a part of the cloud of witnesses that is cheering on to victory those who remain on the earth (Hebrews 12:1). But we must remember that although we are created in the likeness and image of God, and although we are being prepared to receive bodies that will be like the body of our Lord and Savior, we are still individuals who are not omnipresent. Only God is omnipresent.

What do we mean by this? Omnipresent means to be at more than one place at a time, doing an unlimited number of tasks without any one task hindering another. In the same way that the Father, by His Holy Spirit, lives inside of each and every Christian in His fullness, He is still on the throne in heaven seeing all and knowing all. But remember, He is the only one with omnipresence.

What does that mean for the saints? That means we can only be at one place at a time undertaking one task at a time, even in heaven. And because of the greatness, the vastness, and the magnificence of the portion of heaven called Paradise, much time will probably be spent just absorbing and fully realizing the vastness of God.

I'm often asked, "Do you think my loved one is looking on and watching me daily, seeing all the things that I do?" Actually, I don't see that as impossible, but I do see it as highly improbable. We are not omnipresent like God and can only be at one place at a time. I would suspect that their interest will be on the glorious things of God more than the physical things of the earth.

The Changes to Come

Recently, an elderly woman whose daughter passed away, asked me if I thought her daughter would recognize any family members who had died in the past. She also wanted to know what her daughter's eternal body was like.

Questions like this cannot be answered in a few short sentences, and likewise, they should not be answered with some religious cliché. The answers to these questions are found in the Holy Word of God, but let's be clear: The Bible is not to be approached like a dictionary or an encyclopedia where you turn to a certain page and find the answer in one brief statement. Quite the contrary, the Scriptures are to be studied and meditated upon, then revelation comes by the Holy Spirit bringing the answer with peace. Our ability to understand eternity in our earthly thinking is as limited as a child's understanding (1 Corinthians 13:11).

A few years ago, I was talking with some of the children in our children's church. One of the younger girls walked up to me and said in a very childish voice, "Pastor, did you know that I'm going to get a baby brother?" I answered and said, "No, I didn't know that." Then she looked at me with a very serious look on her face and said, "Yes, I am, and I'm really excited because next week we're going to the hospital store to pick one out. I hope he has blonde hair like me!"

Although it was true that the family was going to the hospital the next week, and it was also true that they were bringing home a baby boy, the perception of the five-year-old child was lacking in truthful detail. I'm sure as she matured in later years, the actual truth became more evident to her. Why? Because she grew in knowledge, understanding, and maturity.

At a funeral, many people simply say, "They are in a better place," then they talk about how wonderful heaven is, but deep inside they are full of questions that only study, meditation, and revelation from the Word of God can answer.

When the lady asked me if her daughter would recognize family members in heaven and what her daughter's eternal body would be like, of course I comforted her by saying, "Yes, we will know our families in heaven and in her spirit body, she does have all of her senses, memories, and thoughts." She nodded acknowledgment and left.

I wanted to tell her so much more. I wanted to explain to her that although her daughter was living her eternal life, she was not living in her eternal body. I wanted to tell her of the glorious events yet to take place in her daughter's life. I wanted to help her look forward to the glorious reunion she would someday have with her daughter. It's all detailed in God's book written to us. But there is so much to explain, and it would take time to do that. It would take a lot of time!

As believers, we will move from glory to glory. There will be changes and there will be upgrades. There will be events and there will be a home that Jesus is preparing for each of us. And there will be a day when the New Jerusalem comes down out of heaven and we will occupy our residence. We will have a house within His house. We will have bodies like His body! And when that day comes, it will be just the beginning of a glorious eternity filled with glorious exploration and events. Your next stop—Paradise!

Chapter Two

THE CREATION OF HEAVEN

In the beginning God created the heavens and the earth.

GENESIS 1:1

It is impossible to understand the future plans of God for eternity and His plan for our existence with Him in heaven without an understanding of His greatness and exceedingly unlimited ability to create an existence for us beyond our imagination. If we can begin to comprehend what He has already done in the ancient past, it will assure us that He is able to complete His future promises to us.

"In the beginning God created the heavens and the earth" (Genesis 1:1). In this opening statement of the Bible, we discover a foundational truth: The heavens were created at a specific time in the ancient past. In other words, there was a time when the heavens did not exist. It has been taught that God has forever existed in the eternal past in a place called heaven. However, before the heavens were created, the eternal God of the eternal past existed in His fullness. Before creation, He looked forward through the corridors of time and planned a place and a home for His future creation of man and for Himself.

Science and theology sometimes appear to be in conflict with each other; however, true science and a true understanding of God's plan and His Word do not conflict. At this writing, science teaches that the universe we live in began its existence 13.8 billion years ago with something called the Big Bang. Something unexplainable happened and from a point in non-created matter, there was an explosion ignited from something smaller than an atom. Moving faster than the speed of light (because natural light did not currently exist), this explosion created space and expanded.

Throughout billions of years, this process developed into the universe that we can now see and exist in. Currently, this universe is partially observable. At this writing, it has a known diameter of ninety-four billion light years. With the greatest telescopes we have circling the earth, that's as far as we can see. Although with each upgrade and new telescope launched, we see farther and what do we see? We see more of the same.

Just a century ago, many scientists and astronomers felt that our solar system was the center of the universe. They thought our sun and the planets rotating around it were the main existence and that the stars in the sky were merely for decoration. But as our ability to see deeper into space increased, we discovered that our sun was just one star in a galaxy that contained billions of stars. This galaxy was named the Milky Way and was staggering in its size. Science discovered that it would take 100,000 years to go from one side of the Milky Way to the other side traveling at the speed of light.

One light year is the distance that light traveling at the speed of 186,282.397 miles per second can travel in one year, or simply, one light year is 5.88 trillion miles. The size of the Milky Way was incomprehensible. But as technology increased rapidly, we quickly discovered that the Milky Way, as large as it was, was only one galaxy among many. Although the Milky Way contained billions of suns (stars) with solar systems, we discovered that there were hundreds of billions of other galaxies. At this writing, galaxies are still being discovered at an astounding rate!

True Science and Scripture Do Not Conflict

Science believes that for several hundred million years after the initial spark event (known as the Big Bang theory), the laws of physics (as we know them) were completely absent. There were no photons. Light did not exist.

Then for some unexplained reason (several theories exist), light began to appear. It is also interesting that after the creation of the heavens and the earth were put in motion, God spoke into the darkness and said, "Let there be light," or more accurately, the literal translation from the Hebrew language is, "Light be" (Genesis 1:3).

Although God made the sun, the moon, and the stars on Day 4 of creation, obviously when He said, "Let there be light" on Day 1, He was not referring to light as we know it (traveling at 186,000 miles per second), but He was inserting Himself into the creation process. He was the original Light.

The Apostle John brought forth a very interesting revelation. He said, "...God is light and in Him is no darkness at all" (1 John 1:5). When the New Jerusalem, the holy city of God and the eternal home of the saints, descends from heaven (Revelation 3:12) at the end of the millennium, this city will be illuminated by the mere presence of our Lord (Revelation 21:23). He is the Light of the universe and within His Light there is life.

Many Christians subconsciously limit the creation of God to one rock (the earth), traveling around one star (the sun), in one solar system, never seeing the universe for its massive greatness. It is time for us to understand the infinite grandeur of God's creation. It is time for us to understand that before the heavens and the earth existed, God Almighty existed, and by His Word, everything that was made was made through Him (John 1:3).

The best scientific knowledge of our universe is unable to refute the truth of creation contained in the Word of God. God's Word is true and does not conflict with science.

The Godhead at Creation

In the beginning was the Word, and the Word was with God, and the Word was God. He was in the beginning with God. All things were made through Him, and without Him nothing was made that was made.

JOHN 1:1-3

As we continue reading in the first chapter of John, we find in verse fourteen that the Word became flesh and dwelt with us. In other words, it was the same Word that was in the beginning with God. Here we are clearly told that the Word (Jesus) is God and that through the Word, everything that was created was created through Him. And then to make it even more clear, the Scripture says that without Him (the Word, Jesus) nothing was made that was made.

It is interesting that in Genesis 1:2 we are told that in the beginning the Spirit of God hovered over the face of the waters upon the earth. So, we can clearly determine that in the beginning the Father (God Almighty), the Son (the Word, Jesus), and the Spirit (the Holy Spirit) were all present as one over-seeing the laying of the foundation for the creation of man.

Although the word *trinity* is not in the original text, the concept is. In the beginning the Father, the Son, and the Holy Spirit were all present at creation as one in unity. Also, under-standing the concept of the trinity helps explain the scripture that says, "Let Us make man in Our image according to Our likeness" (Genesis 1:26). Who is God referring to when He says "Us" and "Our"? God is a three-part being (Father, Son, Holy Spirit) (1 John 5:7) and likewise, man is a three-part being (spirit, soul, and body) (1 Thessalonians 5:23).

Although they are one, there is still communication between them. When Jesus was in the garden shortly before His crucifix-ion, He said, "Father, let this cup pass from Me. Nevertheless, not My will, but Thine be done." But in other places when talking to His disciples, Jesus said, "If you've seen Me, you've seen the Father. For the Father and I are one."

These two statements may seem like a paradox and in the natural thinking of man, they are. But in the dimension of the spirit, there is no conflict. God is not bound by the boundaries that surround the physical existence of mankind. God exists outside the framework of physics, time, and matter. Why? Because He is the Creator of all of these entities and He cre-ated them as part of the foundation for the existence of His ultimate creation, the trophy of His grace, the Church.

God Built a House for Man
Before Man was Created

Deep within the soul of every person is a knowing that life is eternal. It has been said that the mind of man cannot comprehend a limitless universe or that there is no beginning to the ancient past. Likewise, within our spirit we know that our existence will never end. The question is not if we will exist, but where will we be? The knowledge that our existence will never end is deep within our spirit because the eternal God created mankind as an eternal spirit. Before the foundation of the world, God had a plan.

Several years ago, I built a home for my family. It was a lengthy process that required planning. First, I purchased a plot of land, then I had architectural drawings made, then the building site had to be prepared with electrical wiring and plumbing. Equipment was eventually brought in and the foundation was dug and concrete poured. All of this took place before the carpenters showed up to build the house. It was a lengthy process, but everything had to be done in a specific order. The last thing that took place was moving my family into the house.

According to God's plan, He wanted to build a house for man, but there was a lot of work to be done first. When God created the universe and this speck in space called Earth, He filled it with all the oxygen, vegetation, minerals, and water that man would need. Because God can see down the corridors of time into the future, He created the seed for an abundance of resources so there would never be lack for mankind (Genesis 1:29-30).

On the day He placed Adam in the Garden of Eden, everything was complete to sustain mankind. All the stars in the heavens, all the resources on the earth, all the ministering angels, and full access to the glory of God were within the grasp of Adam. Adam's job was simply to tend and to keep the garden (Genesis 2:15). In God's grace and kindness, He created the perfect lifestyle for man.

In the beginning God created the heavens and the earth. Notice it doesn't say He created the earth and *then* the heavens. The expanse known as the heavens had a purpose. Before Adam was placed in the garden on the earth, and possibly before the earth was even ready for man, God established a kingdom in heaven. This kingdom had a King who had a throne. As the Creator of the heavens, God was the Supreme Ruler. There was no one like Him (Isaiah 46:5). He had no equal and He has not changed (Malachi 3:6).

> *The LORD has established His throne in heaven, and His kingdom rules over all.*
>
> PSALM 103:19

God does not do anything without a plan. His first creation was the heavens, and the heavens became the foundation for all His future creation. Within His plan was the initial home for man, a garden. In this garden, He planted a seed named Adam, and from this seed God desired a harvest. This harvest would be mankind, created in His image and likeness, and living with Him throughout eternity.

Because of the contamination (sin) of the seed (Adam), it appeared like God's plan was ruined. But the God of love altered His plan which would eventually result in the same ending as His original plan: God and man living together throughout eternity.

The Paradise of God

The word *paradise* in Hebrew and Greek literally means orchard or garden. Originally, before Adam was placed in the garden, the Paradise of God was in heaven. In God's garden, there were other creatures, living beings, heavenly hosts, and angels of varying degrees and function—including Lucifer—who were created to assist God in His plan for mankind.

Lucifer rebelled and was cast out of the Paradise of God to the earth along with one-third of the angels who rebelled with him. Then God prepared a place for man to live: The Garden of Eden. Man lived in the garden until he sinned. After Adam and Eve were driven out of the garden, the next mention of Paradise is in the heart of the earth. It became the abode of the faithful dead and was also known as the bosom of Abraham (Luke 16:22).

The bosom of Abraham should not be confused with another compartment in the earth called Hades. Hades—which is one of the words in the Bible that is commonly referred to as hell—was not created for man, but instead was created for the rebellious devil and his angels (Matthew 25:41). Although Satan's judgment has been sealed, he has not been placed in hell yet. Instead, he has been confined to the earth and its atmosphere until the completion of his sentence is finally executed (Revelation 20:10).

Before Jesus put His blood on the altar in heaven on the day of His resurrection, as we previously mentioned, Paradise was one of the two compartments in the heart of the earth. When Jesus was crucified, there were two thieves being crucified with Him. One thief was nailed to a cross on His left, and the other was nailed to a cross to the right of Him. One of the two thieves mocked and ridiculed Jesus while the other thief acknowledged Him as Lord. Jesus spoke to the second man and said, "Assuredly, I say to you, today you will be with Me in Paradise" (Luke 23:39-43).

Scripture tells us that after Jesus died, He went into the heart of the earth for three days and three nights (Matthew 12:40). While His body was in the tomb, Jesus proclaimed victory to the saints in Paradise and led captivity captive (Ephesians 4:8). After the resurrection of Jesus, Old Testament saints were resurrected (Matthew 27:52-53).

The next time Paradise is mentioned in the Bible, it is in the third heaven. The implication is that the Old Testament saints who were in the bosom of Abraham (Paradise) are now a part of the cloud of witnesses in Paradise in heaven. In the Church age, when the body of a Christian dies, their spirit departs and is escorted into Paradise in heaven where they become a part of the cloud of witnesses.

Paradise is not all inclusive of heaven, it is a specific place in heaven. Much like the heavenly Jerusalem is not all of heaven, it is only a city in heaven.

Summary

Paradise is mentioned in the Bible as being in four different locations. The first location is in heaven before Lucifer rebelled (Ezekiel 28:13). The second mention of Paradise is the Garden of Eden (Genesis 2:8-9). The third location is in the heart of the earth during the time of the Old Covenant (Luke 16:22), and the fourth location is in the third heaven (2 Corinthians 12:2,4). Paradise is again mentioned in the book of Revelation where it is still in heaven. There the tree of life spans the crystal river in the Paradise of God (Revelation 22:2) which will be in the New Jerusalem, the eternal home of the saints.

> *To him who overcomes I will give to eat from the tree*
> *of life, which is in the midst of the Paradise of God.*
>
> REVELATION 2:7

The heavens created by God are vast, and far more expansive than earthly minds could ever imagine, and I am sure there are countless unknown places. But this we know: The heavens created by God are good. They are peaceful and He rules over them. His kingdom reflects Him, and He is love.

Chapter Three

THE HEAVENS
AND BEYOND

When I consider Your heavens, the work of Your fingers,
the moon and the stars, which You have ordained, what
is man that You are mindful of him, and the son of man
that You visit him?

PSALM 8:3-4

When you ask someone, "Where is heaven?" they will usually point upward to the sky. Several times the Bible refers to angels coming down from heaven, and Jesus going up into heaven.

While it is true that the concept of heaven is up, we know that Earth is a globe that rotates, and "up" to a person in China is 180 degrees opposite of up to a person in South Africa. They would literally be pointing in two opposite directions because they are on opposite sides of the globe. However, in twelve hours, up for each of them would reverse.

The truth is that heaven is up for everyone. However, we must think beyond physical directions concerning the location of heaven, because heaven is in a different realm than this physical world.

A foundational truth and the reward for receiving Jesus Christ as our Savior and Lord is eternal life in heaven with the One who created us. But where is this place called heaven? And how can we, as mere humans, understand or even grasp the magnitude of this creation? Is this God (who with His words created the universe with billions of galaxies each containing billions of stars) so lonely that He would see the necessity to create mankind for fellowship? How can we understand His purpose in creation?

First, we must know the truth about the very essence of God Himself. Of course, one of His attributes is that He is the ultimate power, not just in the universe, but beyond the universe. I've heard it said that God inhabits the universe, but His existence is far beyond that. While it is true that He can enter into this universe anywhere and at any time, we must also understand that before the universe existed, He was just as omnipotent and omnipresent as He is now.

Before the universe existed, God spoke, and the spark of creation began. Before the first day of man's time on the earth, God spoke the expanse of the heavens into existence. The God of Creation, the God of Abraham, Isaac, and Jacob, and our God, spoke light in the darkness and the universe began to expand into existence. With all the knowledge that man has acquired, we have never been able to find the end of the universe.

Above the Heavens

In Einstein's Theory of General Relativity and other works, he determined that if matter moved at the speed of light, it would convert into energy and time would cease to exist. Regardless of whether he is right or wrong, if man were able to travel faster than the speed of light (which he is not able to do), he would eventually get to the edge of the universe. How do I know the universe has an end? Because everything that is seen as well as everything that is unseen was created by God (2 Corinthians 4:18). The universe is His creation and like the bowl made of clay by the potter's hand, it has boundaries.

You might ask, "If a person could reach the edge of the universe, what would be there?" It would be the area the Bible calls "far above all the heavens" (Ephesians 4:10). The Bible says that after Jesus was resurrected, He ascended "far above all the heavens." It doesn't say He ascended to the third heaven. It doesn't say He ascended to the seventh heaven. It says He ascended "far above all the heavens," giving us insight to the reality that there is much more unexplored expanse beyond the known universe.

"...He ascended"—what does it mean but that He also first descended into the lower parts of the earth? He who descended is also the One who ascended far above all the heavens, that He might fill all things.

Ephesians 4:9-10

What is "far above all the heavens"? While God resides in heaven (Matthew 6:9), His glory extends far above all the heavens. When Jesus went far above the heavens after His resurrection, He was in the glory of His Father. While heaven itself is an area that we are yet to experience, the area far beyond the heavens is unknown to us. It could contain dimensions beyond our earthly understanding and physics unknown to man. But we do know this: there is an area beyond the heavens where Jesus ascended after His resurrection. In this area is the glory of God.

O LORD, our LORD, how excellent is Your name in all the earth, Who have set Your glory above the heavens!

Psalm 8:1

Could it be that outside of creation, all that exists is simply the glory of God? And could it be that His glory has no boundaries, but rather, is limitless? It certainly is something to think about!

In Psalm 113:4, the Bible tells us that the LORD is high above all nations. Then it goes on to say that His glory is above the heavens.

> *The LORD is high above all nations, His glory above the heavens. Who is like the LORD our God, Who dwells on high?*
>
> PSALM 113:4-5

The Name of God

You will notice in this scripture in Psalms that the word *LORD* is in all capital letters. The purpose is not for emphasis, but to let the reader know that the word used and translated as *LORD* is not actually "LORD," but instead is the sacred holy Hebrew name of God that is unpronounceable. When you see the name "LORD" in the Bible and all four letters are capitalized, it is actually representative of the four Hebrew letters *yod hey vav hey* (יהוה). Some people pronounce this as Yahweh. Some pronounce it as Jehovah, but in reality, it is not to be spoken.

All Hebrew letters have a numeric value. For example, the first of the twenty-two Hebrew letters in the Hebrew alphabet is *aleph* (א) and it has the numeric value of one. The second Hebrew letter is *bet* (ב) that has a numeric value of two. The third letter is *gimel* (ג) that has a numeric value of three. And the fourth letter is *dalet* (ד) that has a numeric value of four. This numbering continues until the twenty-second letter, which is *tav* (ת) that has a numeric value of four hundred.

With this in mind, the name of God, *yod hey vav hey* (יהוה), has a numeric value of twenty-six. This is the reason that the high priest, upon entering the Holy of Holies once a year on the Day of Atonement (Yom Kippur), sprinkled the blood of animals twenty-six times on the lid of the ark of the covenant, which is the mercy seat. He then supernaturally spoke the name of God twenty-six times. God is holy, His name is holy, and the name of God, *yod hey vav hey* (יהוה) is extremely holy.

When the scribes copy the Word of God by hand, they are extremely cautious to copy every letter accurately. Not only do they proofread the text by the letters, they also meticulously convert every letter to its numeric value. Every column and every row on every page must be mathematically accurate, and especially accurate when writing the holy name of God (יהוה). In fact, every time the scribe encounters the name of God in the text, before he can write down "יהוה," he must take a *mikva*, which is a ceremonial bath for cleansing. God is serious about His Word being accurate, and especially serious concerning His name.

With this in mind, looking again at Psalm 113:4, it clearly tells us that the manifestation and glory of the Lord, the Almighty God of Abraham, Isaac, and Jacob, the Creator of the universe, is above the heavens. Then verse five implies strongly that there is none like Him and that He dwells on high. As the Creator of the expanse (at this writing we can see 94 billion light years of it), He is also the Creator of the smallest atomic particles, smaller than protons, neutrons, electrons, and quarks. There is nothing too great or too small that can be hidden from the eyes of Almighty God (Hebrews 4:13).

Why? Because He is the Creator of everything both seen and unseen, both discovered and undiscovered. He is LORD of All.

God's name is extremely holy to Him. God takes His own name very seriously. It is not to be profaned, and it is not to be taken in vain. However, as exalted as His name is, He exalts His Word above His name. This is our assurance that His promises concerning heaven are true and that He will always keep His Word (Titus 1:2).

> *I will worship toward Your holy temple, and praise Your name for Your lovingkindness and Your truth; for You have magnified Your word above all Your name.*
>
> PSALM 138:2

Equal Inheritance

We cannot overstate this truth: God created the universe through His Word and for His Word (Jesus). We must always anchor our understanding of the purpose of eternity to this: God, from outside the universe, created the universe. Although we do not know at this time the full expanse of the universe, we do know Jesus is the Word of God and that by Him and through Him everything that was made (the universe and everything in it) was ultimately to be His possession (Colossians 1:16). Mankind was created to fellowship with Him, but like one-third of the angels in heaven, they rejected Him and separated themselves from Him.

But God, in His love and mercy, knew this would happen before creation, so He devised a plan before the foundation of the world to reconnect His ultimate creation (mankind) to Himself (1 Peter 1:20-21). The new plan was to send His only begotten Son to take the form of a man to lay down His life so that mankind could have life. This act would further show the love and grace of Almighty God.

The universe and everything within it that can be seen and that cannot be seen, God bequeathed by covenant to share with the Body of Christ. Simply stated, God (who created everything through His Son and for His Son) willed His entire inheritance to be equally owned and shared by the Church (1 Peter 1:3-5). The Church has become a joint heir with Jesus (Colossians 1:12).

> *The Spirit Himself bears witness with our spirit that we are children of God, and if children, then heirs— heirs of God and joint heirs with Christ, if indeed we suffer with Him, that we may also be glorified together.*
>
> ROMANS 8:16-17

> *He did this that He might clearly demonstrate through the ages to come the immeasurable (limitless, surpassing) riches of His free grace (His unmerited favor) in [His] kindness and goodness of heart toward us in Christ Jesus.*
>
> EPHESIANS 2:7 (AMPC)

Greater love has no one than this, than to lay down one's life for his friends.

JOHN 15:13

How Many Heavens?

It is interesting to note that the first verse of the Bible says, "In the beginning God created the heavens and the earth." However, I have noticed that many Bible translations say, "heaven and earth" rather than "heavens and earth." Which is correct, and does it really matter? Yes, it matters! In the original Hebrew text, the word *heavens* is plural. So, the correct translation should be "in the beginning God created the heavens and the earth." If that is true (and it is) then how many heavens are there?

Paul said that he was caught up into the third heaven and he didn't know if he was in his body or out of his body. But either way, what he did know was that he went to the third heaven. Now it stands to reason that if there is a third heaven, then there is a first and a second heaven as well.

> *I was caught up to the third heaven fourteen years ago. Whether I was in my body or out of my body, I don't know—only God knows. Yes, only God knows whether I was in my body or outside my body. But I do know that I was caught up to paradise and heard*

things so astounding that they cannot be expressed in words, things no human is allowed to tell.
2 Corinthians 12:2-4 (NLT)

In the canonized Scriptures that are considered to be the Holy Bible, there are only three heavens mentioned. The first heaven is the atmosphere that envelops the earth. In ancient times it was thought to extend to the level of the tallest mountain. The second heaven is what we now call outer space. In the third heaven is Paradise. Is there evidence of more than three heavens?

Evidence in the Dead Sea Scrolls

Sometime between November 1946 and February 1947, three Bedouin shepherds discovered seven scrolls housed in jars in a cave near Qumran, Israel. They took with them a handful of scrolls that included the Isaiah scroll and the Habakkuk commentary. They took the scrolls back to the camp to show their family and, thankfully, none of the scrolls were destroyed in the process. The Bedouins kept these scrolls hanging on a tent pole, periodically taking them to display them to their tribe.

They tried to sell the scrolls to a dealer in Bethlehem, but he returned them, saying they were worthless. He said this because he feared they may have been stolen from a synagogue. Undaunted by this, the shepherds went to a market and found a Syrian Christian who offered to buy them. The original scrolls changed hands, and some were sold for very low prices.

The rediscovery of the Qumran caves started in 1949 by the Jordanian Department of Antiquities. Since then, several other caves have been discovered with a total of 972 manuscripts having been found. About forty percent of the documents are copies of texts from Hebrew Scriptures. Another thirty percent are texts from the second temple period which were not canonized in the Hebrew Bible. This includes the Book of Enoch, the Book of Jubilees, the Book of Tobit, the Wisdom of Sirach, Psalms 152-155, and several others. The remaining thirty percent of the scrolls are manuscripts of previously unknown documents that shed light on the rules of groups within Judaism.

Among these scrolls was the Testament of Levi, which gives us some insight into the number of heavens. The custom of the ancient patriarchs was to write down their knowledge of God along with the times when God had spoken to them. As their physical departure was imminent, they would gather their families together and read to them their testament and then pass it on to their children. Levi recorded in his testament that there were seven heavens and described what is in each one.

Levi's father was Jacob whose name was changed to Israel. Jacob's twelve sons became the twelve tribes of Israel and Levi was the father of the tribe of Levi. Levi's grandfather was Isaac and his great-grandfather was Abraham. The Bible tells us

God spoke to all of them and all of this knowledge would have been passed down to Levi. So even though the Testament of Levi is not considered to be Scripture, we should consider its authenticity and understand that the patriarchs believed there were seven heavens.

The important thing for us to remember is this: there are multiple heavens but only one Earth. The boundaries of the heavens are not yet known, but the city, the New Jerusalem, our eternal home, will come down from there (Revelation 21:2). Regardless of how many heavens there are, God created them all.

Chapter Four

THE CITY OF GOD

But now they desire a better, that is, a heavenly country.
Therefore, God is not ashamed to be called their God,
for He has prepared a city for them.

HEBREWS 11:16

Heaven is a beautiful place and the extent of its beauty cannot
be described in an earthly language. When Paul visited the third
heaven, he heard words that were inexpressible. Heaven is truly
a place that is so far beyond the physical reality in which we
now live that to adequately describe it would be futile. However,
the Bible does give us a glimpse into its beauty and expanse.

While the Bible gives us the size and dimensions of the
New Jerusalem, the totality of heaven itself is not given. The
extent of its boundaries is unknown to us. At the time of this
writing, science has not yet discovered the boundaries of our

physical universe that God created, and the place called heaven is infinitely greater. All through the Scriptures we discover that the spiritual existence is the true original existence and everything that we see, touch, and feel has been created out of what we cannot see.

> *While we do not look at the things which are seen, but at the things which are not seen. For the things which are seen are temporary, but the things which are not seen are eternal.*
> 2 CORINTHIANS 4:18

But we do know this: heaven is a kingdom and within the kingdom of heaven there is a King who rules over the entire kingdom. Within the kingdom there are cities. Cities have rulers that rule at the king's pleasure. The Bible tells us that in the future there will be those who will rule and reign with Jesus from heaven (Revelation 1:5-6). Jesus even said that some will rule over larger domains than others (Luke 19:11-19). The implication from this is that there could possibly be cities scattered throughout the place called heaven.

But we know for sure that when the New Jerusalem arrives at the end of the millennium, it will be the crown jewel of heaven and the center of all authority. If there are other cities in heaven, none will equal it!

The heavenly Jerusalem is the place of the original temple of God that contains the heavenly Holy of Holies. Within the Holy of Holies is the mercy seat which is actually the lid of the ark of the covenant that has two cherubim on it facing each other with their wings outstretched.

This is where Jesus placed His blood on the day of His resurrection and became the firstborn among many brethren (Romans 8:29), the firstfruits of the kingdom (1 Corinthians 15:23), and took His place as the head of the Church (Colossians 1:18). For mankind, the greatest miracle of all eternity was when the first drop of the blood of Jesus touched the altar. He paid the price once for all eternity, so that man could live (Hebrews 7:27). Without this event, mankind was destined for an eternity separated from the goodness of God. Without this event, the glorious Church could not exist. This one event changed everything!

The Heavenly Jerusalem Will Become the New Jerusalem

But you have come to Mount Zion and to the city of the living God, the heavenly Jerusalem, to an innumerable company of angels.

HEBREWS 12:22

Then I, John, saw the holy city, New Jerusalem, coming down out of heaven from God, prepared as a bride adorned for her husband.

REVELATION 21:2

Before we go any further, we need to make the distinction between the heavenly Jerusalem and the New Jerusalem. While both are the dwelling place of God the Father, and both are the dwelling place of the saints, they do not exist simultaneously. The heavenly Jerusalem has been in existence from the creation of the heavens and is the heavenly capital city that is in existence now. This heavenly city will continue until the end of the millennium, until after the great white throne judgment, and until after death has been totally defeated for all eternity.

Then the New Jerusalem will descend out of heaven upon the earthly Jerusalem (Revelation 21:2). This is the place that is the home of God and it is the place that Jesus is preparing for those who believe. The New Jerusalem will be the eternal home of the saints (Revelation 21:9). While the saints of God will have their home base in this new city, travel beyond comprehension and discoveries beyond our current understanding will be available.

The main distinction between the heavenly Jerusalem and the New Jerusalem is their placement in time.

Another major distinction between the heavenly Jerusalem and the New Jerusalem is that the heavenly Jerusalem that exists currently has a temple in it, but there will be no temple in the New Jerusalem. Within the temple in the heavenly Jerusalem is the original ark of the covenant that was placed there from the beginning. The sole purpose of the heavenly ark of the covenant was to accept the blood of Jesus when He became the perfect sacrifice.

Then the temple of God was opened in heaven, and the ark of His covenant was seen in His temple. And there were lightnings, noises, thunderings, an earthquake, and great hail.

REVELATION 11:19

When Moses was on Mount Sinai receiving the commandments from God for the Hebrew people, he like Paul, was taken to heaven. Moses was shown the heavenly temple and given the dimensions and instructions on how to build a replica of the heavenly ark on the earth. When the construction of the ark was completed on the earth, it was merely a copy of the original in heaven. While the earthly ark continually received the blood of bulls and goats as a shadow of sin being covered, the heavenly ark waited for the sacrifice of the Son of God to receive the blood of the Son of Man.

Who serve the copy and shadow of the heavenly things, as Moses was divinely instructed when he was about to make the tabernacle. For He said, "See that you make all things according to the pattern shown you on the mountain."

HEBREWS 8:5

The earthly ark required a continual sacrifice because the removal of sin was never complete. Even on Yom Kippur, the Day of Atonement, when the high priest would enter into the Holy of Holies and sprinkle the blood and say the name of God twenty-six times, it was never enough. The blood of

bulls and goats on the earthly ark was a never-ending proce-
dure. However, when Jesus placed His blood on the original
ark (mercy seat) in heaven, He did it one time (Hebrews 9:12).
His perfect blood on the perfect ark stopped the need for sacrifice. Its function was complete.

> *For Christ has not entered the holy places made with
> hands, which are copies of the true, but into heaven
> itself, now to appear in the presence of God for us.*
>
> HEBREWS 9:24

The things that were in the temple on the earth were mere
copies of what was in the temple in heaven. In fact, we are
told in Hebrews they were mere copies of what was shown
to Moses. It's good to note that a copy is not of the quality of
the original. Everything in heaven is perfect. The blood that
Jesus put on the altar in heaven was perfect and the altar was
perfect. It had never had blood placed on it before. It was created when the heavens were created, waiting through the eons
of time for the perfect blood to be placed on it. Remember,
before the creation of man and before the foundation of the
world, it was ordained that Jesus would be the once-and-for-
all perfect sacrifice.

> *He then would have had to suffer often since the foun-
> dation of the world; but now, once at the end of the*

ages, He has appeared to put away sin by the sacrifice of Himself.

HEBREWS 9:26

On the other hand, we are clearly told in Revelation 21 that the New Jerusalem does not have a temple, which means there is no ark in the Holy of Holies. Why? It is really very simple. At that time, there will be no need for an ark, no need for a mercy seat, and no longer a need for a place for a blood sacrifice. It's over. It's done. It's complete! The price has been paid in full and for all eternity. The Son will be the glory of the New Jerusalem. The Son will be the Sun.

> *But I saw no temple in it, for the LORD God Almighty and the Lamb are its temple. The city had no need of the sun or of the moon to shine in it, for the glory of God illuminated it. The Lamb is its light.*

REVELATION 21:22-23

Earth, an Image of the Original

> *By faith we understand that the worlds were framed by the word of God, so that the things which are seen were not made of things which are visible.*

HEBREWS 11:3

In the beginning God created the heavens and the earth, and we are told that everything He created was good. The land, the oceans, the plant life, the animal life were all created perfect. The beauty and majesty of the planet Earth was unparalleled (Genesis 1:31). There was nothing like it anywhere else in the universe. The God who created the universe created a peaceful landscape where there was peace and tranquility. Before sin entered and everything became cursed, the earth was a paradise.

Since the physical world that we live in is only an image of the unseen world of the spirit, we can only imagine the beauty and majesty of what we can't now see in heaven. I have traveled this earth and have seen the great beauty of our oceans. New Zealand, Australia, Hawaii, Israel, and the Mediterranean are places where I have seen the beauty of the seas and the seashore, but nothing on earth can compare to the beauty of the crystal sea at the throne of God and the crystal river that flows from the throne.

Before the throne there was a sea of glass, like crystal.
REVELATION 4:6

And he showed me a pure river of water of life, clear as crystal, proceeding from the throne of God and of the Lamb.
REVELATION 22:1

There are beautiful trees throughout the world—the giant redwoods of California, the mighty oak trees, as well as the olive trees of Israel. Although the trees have great beauty, they don't even come close in comparison to the tree of life that hovers over the crystal river in heaven.

In the middle of its street, and on either side of the river, was the tree of life, which bore twelve fruits, each tree yielding its fruit every month. The leaves of the tree were for the healing of the nations.

REVELATION 22:2

Two Jerusalems

In all the earth there is only one parcel of land that was set aside by God for His chosen people. Within that land, there is a city that has been chosen to be the ruling capital of the earth. Within that city, there is a place where the greatest historical events of all time have taken place. This place is the Temple Mount.

Satan hates the Temple Mount and the city of Jerusalem. It represents the power of God and the location of his prophesied defeat. This small mountain in a very small city is the focal point of daily international news. Satan has always and will always attempt to take control of this precious parcel of land. Even though his failure and destiny are sealed, like a rabid dog he insanely attempts to conquer and control, not accepting that he has been judged and his fate cannot be changed.

God loves and honors Jerusalem and the Temple Mount. It is the place where He gathered the soil and created man. It is the place that Abraham took Isaac to be sacrificed. It is the place where Jacob, who was sleeping with a rock for his pillow, saw heavenly angels traveling to and from heaven. It was the threshing floor that was purchased by King David. It is the place of Solomon's Temple, and the second temple, and will be the location of the temple to come.[1] It was the place where Jesus was circumcised. It is the place where the Antichrist will attempt to exalt himself as God (2 Thessalonians 2:3-4). The history of mankind started in Jerusalem and will continue throughout eternity from there.

The Hebrew word for Jerusalem is *Yerushalayim*. Hebrew words ending in "ayim" do not designate plurality, they designate two of something. Within the name of Jerusalem, it is stated that there are two Jerusalems.

Once, while in the Old City of Jerusalem I noticed that several murals of the city also had an image of a city in the clouds above it. In fact, for many years, a mural like this hung in the Israeli Prime Minister's office. When I asked a rabbi about this, his response was, "We have always known that there are two Jerusalems. There is the earthly Jerusalem and the heavenly Jerusalem."

Jerusalem is built as a city that is compact together.
PSALM 122:3

There will be a day when the earthly Jerusalem will be restored beyond its former glory and the boundaries of Israel will be as prophesied in Ezekiel 47. After the enemy is defeated at the end of the tribulation, the resurrection of the righteous Jews will take place as prophesied in Daniel 12:1-2. These resurrected Jews will live in earthly bodies along with the righteous Jews that survived the tribulation. They will live in Israel and Jerusalem will be the capital of the world. Longevity will be restored (Isaiah 65:20).

During the millennium, the nations of the world will pay tribute to Israel. If they don't, it will bring a curse upon them. This is the fulfillment of the scripture that says, those who bless Israel will be blessed and those who curse Israel will be cursed (Genesis 12:3).

Jesus Christ will be the ultimate King and Ruler over planet Earth and this rulership will continue for one thousand years. While the Jews and the nation of Israel are ruling the world in natural human bodies, the Church (having been raptured seven years before) will also be ruling and reigning in glorified bodies from the heavenly Jerusalem. Overseeing all of these sub-rulers will be Jesus Christ the King.

While these two cities are separate, they are one. One is on the earth and one is above it in the heavens. They are 'Yerushalayim.'

The New Jerusalem—New and Improved

At the end of the one-thousand-year rule, after the enemy experiences total defeat and destruction, and after the great white throne judgment (and the devil and death are no more), God performs a great creative event: He creates a new heaven, a new earth, and a New Jerusalem (Isaiah 65:17-19).

> *Now I saw a new heaven and a new earth, for the first heaven and the first earth had passed away. Also there was no more sea. Then I, John, saw the holy city, New Jerusalem, coming down out of heaven from God, prepared as a bride adorned for her husband.*
>
> REVELATION 21:1-2

In the Greek New Testament (Textus Receptus), there are two words translated "new" in our English Bible. They are *neos* and *kainos*. *Neos* means "new in time, something that has never been in existence before." *Kainos* means "new in nature or something that has been refurbished and improved."

In Revelation 21:1, the Greek word used for a new heaven, a new earth, and New Jerusalem is *kainos*. The new heaven, the new earth, and the New Jerusalem are not a different heaven, a different earth, and a different heavenly Jerusalem, but they are all restored, refurbished, and upgraded to brand-new condition.

John was approached in his vision by one of the seven angels who had the seven bowls with the seven plagues. The angel said to him, "Come, and I will show you the bride, the Lamb's wife." Then John was taken away by the Holy Spirit to a very high mountain. While standing there, he saw the great city, the holy Jerusalem descending out of heaven, covered with the glory of God.

Then one of the seven angels who had the seven bowls filled with the seven last plagues came to me and talked with me, saying, "Come, I will show you the bride, the Lamb's wife." And he carried me away in the Spirit to a great and high mountain, and showed me the great city, the holy Jerusalem, descending out of heaven from God.

REVELATION 21:9-10

The Bride of Christ is the Church

Because the angel said, "Come, I will show you the bride, the Lamb's wife," and then he showed John the New Jerusalem descending from heaven, some have used this statement to say that the new city of Jerusalem is, in fact, the Bride of Christ.

First, it should be noted that when people refer to a city that they like or dislike, they are not referring to buildings and structures but rather to the people who inhabit that city.

Additionally, the Scriptures clearly tell us that the Bride of Christ is the Church, the assembly of born-again believers. Ephesians 5:25 states that husbands should love their wives in the same way that Christ loved the Church and gave Himself for her. The marriage supper of the Lamb (which takes place *before* the millennial kingdom begins), cannot include a city that does not appear until after the millennium is concluded. Jesus is not marrying buildings, walls, and rooms, but He will be united with those who believe, as He requested when talking to His Father in John chapter 17. The Bride of Christ is the Church.

A Description of the New City

In his vision, John the Apostle said that the New Jerusalem, the holy city, glowed. He described it as a light that was like a precious jasper stone, but clear as crystal. Then he saw that surrounding the city was a very great, high wall with twelve gates. There was an angel at each gate and each one had a name written upon it. The twelve names on the twelve gates were the names of the twelve tribes of the children of Israel. Three gates were on the east, three gates were on the north, three gates on the south, and three gates were on the west (Revelation 21:11-13).

Remember, we are talking about a city in heaven, not the entirety of heaven. The wall of the city had twelve foundations upon which were the names of the twelve apostles of the Lamb. As John was walking and talking with his guide, he was handed a gold reed and was told to measure the city, the gates, and its wall. When he did, he discovered that the city itself was laid out in a perfect square. The height, the width, and the length were all the same measurement (Revelation 21:14-16).

The Bible says that the length, width, and height were each 12,000 *furlongs*. In the original manuscripts, the word translated as furlong was actually the Greek word *stadia*. Twelve thousand stadia is about 1,380 miles, and some translate it as 1,500 miles. The size of the city is so massive that if it were hovering over North America, it would cover almost half of the continental United States.

Keep in mind, it is also described as 1,500 miles high! How high is this? Think of it this way. The International Space Station in outer space is only two hundred twenty miles above the earth. The New Jerusalem will extend seven times farther into space than the space station. If a building in the New Jerusalem was built to the full height of the city, it would have about 646,000 floors. That's a lot of buttons to push on an elevator! But, of course, we won't need elevators then!

When John went on to describe the beauty of the city, he described the walls, the gates, and the streets of the city as very precious stones, pearls, and gold (Revelation 21:17-21).

The Bible describes the inhabitants of the city by saying that they will bring into the city the glory and the honor of the nations. Nothing unclean will ever enter into the city of the New Jerusalem, but only those whose names are written in the Lamb's Book of Life will enter (Revelation 21:27).

The Purpose of the Leaves on the Tree of Life

In the middle of its street, and on either side of the river, was the tree of life, which bore twelve fruits,

*each tree yielding its fruit every month. The leaves of
the tree were for the healing of the nations.*

REVELATION 22:2

This verse implies that sickness and disease will still exist
for the people who are living in the Gentile nations during the
millennium. Otherwise, the nations of the earth would not need
to partake of the leaves of the tree of life in order to be healed.

Because Jesus died and became the perfect sacrifice, He
eliminated sin for all who would believe in Him during the
Church age. As we stated earlier, the Church will be raptured and given glorified bodies. These glorified bodies will
never age, nor have any sickness, disease, or anything harm-
ful throughout eternity.

However, there will still be a civilization that will be living
on the earth in human bodies. These will be people who were
saved from the destruction of the tribulation, or were resurrected
after the tribulation, or their descendants. Simply restated,
these human bodies will need healing; otherwise, the tree of
life that supplies leaves for healing of the nations would not
be necessary. Access to the tree of life by the nations is determined by whether or not they bless Israel. His commandment
is that Israel is to be blessed.

*And it shall come to pass that everyone who is left of
all the nations which came against Jerusalem shall go
up from year to year to worship the King, the LORD of*

hosts, and to keep the Feast of Tabernacles. And it shall be that whichever of the families of the earth do not come up to Jerusalem to worship the King, the LORD *of hosts, on them there will be no rain.*

ZECHARIAH 14:16-17

Blessed are those who do His commandments, that they may have the right to the tree of life, and may enter through the gates into the city.

REVELATION 22:14

God's Plan for the Temple

Before the foundation of the world, God foreknew that His ultimate creation (mankind) would fail. But His love for the world was so great that He instituted a plan for man to be redeemed before man was ever created (Ephesians 1:4). After the failure of man in the garden, God began to teach mankind about His plan for the future. One of His methods of teaching was to have earthly structures constructed that resembled things in heaven.

As we said earlier, God showed Moses the altar in heaven that would eventually have the blood of Jesus placed upon it. He instructed Moses to build a copy of it on the earth. Through the earthly copy, God trained and taught His people the purpose of a blood covenant. On the day of Jesus' resurrection, He placed His precious blood on the altar in heaven that Moses had observed. By placing His blood on the altar that was in the Holy of Holies in the temple in the heavenly Jerusalem, it eliminated the need for a future temple in heaven.

So, what is the purpose today of the temple in the heavenly Jerusalem? It is simply the showcase where the blood of Jesus is on display for all the universe to see. It continually proclaims the work has been done for the elimination of sin in the Body of Christ, and it is evidence to the enemy proclaiming his eternal defeat. The blood of Jesus will be on display in this temple until the final victory is proclaimed at the end of the millennium and death is no more. At that time, there will no longer be a need for the display, thus eliminating the need for the temple and the sacrificial altar. For all eternity there will never be the need for another sacrifice.

Before we can completely understand why there will be no need for a temple after the millennium, we must look to the past. While the study of the previous temples may seem tedious and even boring to some, we must remember that they were given to the Hebrews as an example or template of our future. Through meditation of the Word concerning these historical structures, the Holy Spirit will give revelation and insight to our future home. A full understanding of the future is impossible without a complete understanding of the past.

Solomon's Temple

The First Temple

Solomon, the son of King David, took the nation of Israel into a time of great prosperity. He also oversaw the construction of the temple before its destruction by Nebuchadnezzar II after the siege of Jerusalem in 587 BC.

The Bible states that the temple was constructed under Solomon while he ruled over the United Kingdom of Israel and Judah. The temple housed the ark of the covenant. The Jewish historian Josephus tells us that, "The temple was burnt 470 years, six months, and ten days after it was built."

In the Book of 1 Kings we are told of the temple's dedication. When the priests emerged from the Holy of Holies after placing the ark there, the temple was filled with an overpowering cloud, the shekinah glory of God, which interrupted the dedication ceremony.

> *And it came to pass, when the priests came out of the holy place, that the cloud filled the house of the LORD, so that the priests could not continue ministering because of the cloud; for the glory of the LORD filled the house of the LORD.*
>
> 1 KINGS 8:10-11

After leading the entire assembly of Israel in prayer, Solomon noted that the construction of the temple represented a fulfillment of God's promise to David. The temple was dedicated as a place of prayer and reconciliation for the people of Israel and for those living there who were from other nations. At the conclusion of the dedication, 22,000 bulls and 120,000 sheep were sacrificed.

Inside the first temple was an area called the Holy of Holies, or Kodesh haKodashim in Hebrew. This inner sanctuary was floored and wainscoted with cedars of Lebanon and its walls and floor were overlaid with gold amounting to 600 talents or roughly twenty metric tons (1 Kings 6:16,20). In the inner sanctuary were two cherubim made of olive wood and overlaid with gold. Each was ten cubits high, having a wingspan of ten cubits. When they stood side by side, their wings touched the wall on either side and met at the center of the room (1 Kings 6:23-28). There was a two-leaved door between them and the holy place was overlaid with gold. Also, there was a veil of tekhelet (blue), purple, crimson, and fine linen (2 Chronicles 3:14). There were no windows. It was considered to be the dwelling place of the name of God.

Within the Kodesh haKodashim (the Holy of Holies) was the resting place of the ark of the covenant. When the temple was dedicated, the ark that contained the original tablets of the Ten Commandments was placed beneath the cherubim. The ark had two golden cherubim with their wings outstretched covering the lid of the ark, also known as the mercy seat (Exodus 25:18-20).

The porch (Ulam) was the entrance before the temple on the east side. It was twenty cubits long and ten cubits deep, and on it stood two pillars (Jachin and Boaz) which were eighteen cubits high (1 Kings 7:21).

Two courts surrounded the temple—the inner court and the great court. The inner court (1 Kings 6:36) was known as the Court of the Priests (2 Chronicles 4:9). It contained the Altar of burnt-offering, the Brazen Sea Laver, along with ten other lavers. A brazen altar stood before the temple.

The great court surrounded the entire temple and it was the place where the general assembly stood to worship (Jeremiah 19:14; Jeremiah 26:2).

The Molten Sea, also known as the Brazen Sea, was a large basin in the temple used for the ceremonial act of washing parts of the body by the priests. This basin was supplied by water brought by way of a conduit from Solomon's pools. Josephus, in his writings *Antiquities of the Jews,* recorded that the vessels of the temple were composed of orichalcum (a form of brass or alloy) and covered in gold.

Nebuchadnezzar besieged Jerusalem, and after thirty months, he breeched the walls in 587 BC. The temple was destroyed on Tisha B'Av, the 9th day of Av on the Hebrew calendar.

Herod's Temple

The Second Temple

Herod's Temple, known as the second temple, stood on Temple Mount from 516 BC to 70 AD. The second temple was originally a very modest structure that was constructed by Jewish exiles who returned from Babylon under the governor Zerubbabel. However, during the reign of Herod the Great, the temple was completely overhauled and refurbished. The Romans destroyed the second temple in 70 AD as retaliation for a Jewish rebellion. The second temple existed a total of 585 years.

During the time of the second temple, there were several significant events that took place. One of these occurred in 167 BC when Antiochus IV Epiphanes built an altar to Zeus in the temple. He also banned circumcision, and then as a final desecration, he ordered that pigs be sacrificed on the holy altar in the temple. After the Maccabean Revolt against the Seleucid Empire, the second temple was rededicated.

The reconstruction of this temple under Herod began in 20 BC and ended in 10 BC. This construction project was the largest of the first century. The historian Josephus records that Herod was most interested in building a name for himself through this project which was paid for by heavy taxation. The old temple built by Zerubbabel was replaced by Herod's edifice.

The Third Temple

One of my favorite places to go in Israel is the Temple Institute. The Temple Institute is an organization that is preparing for the construction of the third temple. In Revelation

11 we are given the measurements of a temple that will exist in Jerusalem during the time of the Great Tribulation.

> *Then I was given a reed like a measuring rod. And the angel stood, saying, "Rise and measure the temple of God, the altar, and those who worship there. But leave out the court which is outside the temple, and do not measure it, for it has been given to the Gentiles. And they will tread the holy city underfoot for forty-two months. And I will give power to my two witnesses, and they will prophesy one thousand two hundred and sixty days, clothed in sackcloth."*
>
> REVELATION 11:1-3

This scripture shows us that another temple will exist on Temple Mount. We know from the prophecies in Daniel 9:27 and Matthew 24:15 that a temple must exist during the time of tribulation, before Jesus returns to the earth at the Mount of Olives (the Second Coming) to defeat the Antichrist, bind Satan, and set up His millennial kingdom. There are several other prophecies that confirm this. Second Thessalonians 2:4 says that the man of lawlessness will set himself up in the temple and proclaim himself to be God. For this to happen, there must be a third temple in place.

Ezekiel's Temple

In Ezekiel chapters 40 to 48, a temple is described that is a size that has never existed. The Bible is unclear if the third temple will become the millennial temple or if a fourth temple will be built. The size of the temple that Ezekiel describes is so much greater than any previous temple that it would not even fit on Mount Moriah. In fact, if it's built to specifications, much of Jerusalem would need to be rearranged to meet the specifications.

When Jesus returns at the Second Coming, we do know that there will be a great earthquake that splits the Mount of Olives (Zechariah 14:4). This earthquake also splits the city of Jerusalem and could conceivably destroy the third temple and reformat the entire landscape of Jerusalem and the surrounding area. By the sheer magnitude of the size of Ezekiel's Temple, the implication is that it will be a fourth temple and not a refurbished third temple.

There Will Be No Temple in the New Jerusalem

But I saw no temple in it, for the Lord God Almighty and the Lamb are its temple.
REVELATION 21:22

One of the most interesting aspects of the New Jerusalem is that it has no temple. And, as we discussed earlier, the Son will be the illumination of the New Jerusalem.

It cannot be overstated that there will be no need for a temple in eternity. To have a temple with a sacrificial altar would imply that the sacrifice of the Lamb of God, our Lord and Savior Jesus Christ, was insufficient, lacking, or incomplete. It would also suggest that an additional sacrifice could possibly be necessary in the future. To have a temple with an altar in the New Jerusalem would be an insult and dishonor to the sacrifice that Jesus made. The Lord God Almighty and the Lamb are its temple.

The most important day in all of history for mankind was the day that the perfect blood of Jesus was placed on the perfect altar in heaven, the price being paid in full for the redemption of mankind. Without this sacrifice, man was destined to an eternity of separation from God. The price was paid in full, and therefore, there will be no need for a sacrificial altar.

> *Not with the blood of goats and calves, but with His own blood, He entered the Most Holy Place once for all, having obtained eternal redemption.*
>
> HEBREWS 9:12

The Lord's Prayer Fulfilled

In John 17, in His prayer to the Father shortly before His crucifixion, Jesus spoke of being one with the Father, and of those who would believe in Him being one with Him *and* the Father.

> *I do not pray for these alone, but also for those who will believe in Me through their word; that they all may be one, as You, Father, are in Me, and I in You; that they*

*also may be one in Us, that the world may believe that
You sent Me. And the glory which You gave Me I have
given them, that they may be one just as We are one: I
in them, and You in Me; that they may be made perfect
in one, and that the world may know that You have
sent Me, and have loved them as You have loved Me.*

JOHN 17:20-23

Paul, in his letter to the Corinthians, made another interesting statement. He said that their individual bodies were the temple of the Holy Spirit. Nowhere in Scripture is there any indication that the Church will cease from being the habitation of the Spirit of God.

*Do you not know that your body is the temple of the
Holy Spirit who is in you, whom you have from God,
and you are not your own?*

1 CORINTHIANS 6:19

In eternity future, when all the judgments and prophecies have been fulfilled and we are living in our eternal home in the New Jerusalem, the desire Jesus expressed in His prayer to the Lord before His execution and resurrection will be completely fulfilled. For eternity, throughout the heavens the Spirit of God will be living inside of glorified mankind. Then man will truly be one with the Father and the Son.

Some may say, "We are one with Him now." In a sense, that is true in that we who believe have the Holy Spirit living within us, but we are still in earthen vessels that have not been glorified. The fullness of the prophetic desire of Jesus will be fulfilled after the completion of our glorification and the last victory over death has been accomplished.

> *Then comes the end, when He delivers the kingdom to God the Father, when He puts an end to all rule and all authority and power. For He must reign till He has put all enemies under His feet. The last enemy that will be destroyed is death.*
>
> 1 CORINTHIANS 15:24-26

With God there are special dates and special places that He has reserved as His own. He has designated them as holy. On these dates and in these places, there is to be holiness and worship. One such place is the holy city of Jerusalem. In Psalm 46 the Kohathites, who were an important branch of singers and the sons of Korah (the cousin of Moses), sang of the holy city and called it the holy place of the tabernacle of the Most High.

Throughout the Holy Scriptures it has been made clear that Jerusalem is the city of God and a holy place. This holy city on the earth connected to the holy city in heaven will forever be the ruling capital of the earth and the universe.

> *There is a river whose streams shall make glad the city of God, the holy place of the tabernacle of the Most High.*
>
> PSALM 46:4

Endnote

1. Israel Ariel and Chaim Richman, *Carta's Illustrated Encyclopedia of the Holy Temple in Jerusalem*, (Israel: The Temple Institute and Carta, Jerusalem, 2005), pages 2, 4, 5, 6, 18.

Chapter Five

KEYS TO UNDERSTANDING

Be diligent to present yourself approved to God, a worker who does not need to be ashamed, rightly dividing the word of truth.

2 TIMOTHY 2:15

We are told in the Bible that when we study the Word, we should rightly divide it. If the Word can be rightly divided, then obviously it can also be wrongly divided. So, the obvious question is, "How do I rightly divide the Word of God?"

In order to fully understand the Scriptures referring to the end of days and our journey to heaven, you must know that every scripture is relevant to the Church; however, every scripture is not speaking to the Church or about the Church. With that in mind, the following four basic principles will help unlock the mysteries hidden within many scriptures.

Four Basic Principles

There are four basic principles that must be understood before the Word of God can be rightly divided. Without an understanding of these four principles, you cannot clearly understand New Testament teaching in its fullness. Most biblical misunderstanding comes from a lack of comprehension of these four basic principles.

1. You are a three-part being—spirit, soul, and body.
2. Righteousness and holiness are not the same thing.
3. There are currently three groups of people on the earth.
4. With the Lord, one day is as a thousand years, and a thousand years as one day.

1. *Spirit, Soul, and Body*

> *Now may the God of peace Himself sanctify you completely; and may your whole spirit, soul, and body be preserved blameless at the coming of our Lord Jesus Christ.*
>
> 1 THESSALONIANS 5:23

Your spirit is the real you and is eternal (Matthew 25:46). When you are saved, it is your spirit that is born again (1 Peter 1:23). At salvation, your spirit becomes a born-again, new creation. All things become new, and old things pass away (2

Corinthians 5:17). At the moment you are born again, your spirit is made righteous and the Holy Spirit of God moves permanently within your born-again spirit (2 Corinthians 5:21; 1 Corinthians 3:16). After salvation, your spirit can no longer sin because it is possessed by the Spirit of God (1 John 3:9). God is light and in Him is no darkness (1 John 1:5). Your born-again spirit is renewed daily by God, sealed by the Holy Spirit until the day of redemption (2 Corinthians 4:16; Ephesians 4:30; Ephesians 1:13).

Your soul is your mind, your will, your intellect, and your emotions. It is the gateway to your spirit and heart. Your soul is not born again, and you must choose to daily renew your soul with the Word (Romans 12:2). Your soul decides whether you are led by the Holy Spirit, your spirit, or by your flesh (your five senses). Your soul is not made righteous when your spirit is born again but becomes holy through obedience to the Word of God (Hebrews 12:14).

Your body is simply the earthly container your spirit lives in and can only function when a spirit is living within it. The body does not make choices, but is subject to the will of the soul. However, if the soul allows addictions within the body, a person can become ruled by the flesh. Your earthly body will either cease to work and decay, or it will be caught up in the rapture. At the rapture, the bodies of all born-again believers, living or dead, will be changed into glorified bodies that will be possessed by their born-again spirits (1 Corinthians 15:51-54).

2. *Righteousness and Holiness Are Not the Same Thing*

Righteousness and holiness are often confused, and the terms are sometimes used interchangeably, but righteousness and holiness are not the same. Although they have many of the same characteristics, and even though a Christian can have both, they are different in how they are attained and how we function within them.

Righteousness is a gift (Romans 5:17). Holiness is a choice (Hebrews 12:14). To think the terms *righteous* and *holy* are the same thing brings confusion to the Scriptures making it difficult to understand our place in Christ.

Righteousness is a gift of God, not a result of any work that man can do. Holiness is not a gift from God, but a decision of obedience by man. God supplies the grace, man supplies the submission with obedience to the Word of God, and holiness is the result. Righteousness is a result of the act of God, while holiness is a result of the acts of men by their own free will.

Righteousness is simply being in proper relationship with God. At the moment in time that our spirit is renewed, we become righteous. Righteousness is not something we have; it is something we are.

> For as by one man's disobedience many were made sinners, so also by one Man's obedience many will be made righteous.
>
> ROMANS 5:19

Holiness is something that we develop. The spirit is made righteous and guides the soul toward holiness. Most people, after becoming a Christian, are not very holy. Many old habits and addictions still exist after being born again. Holiness has nothing to do with our salvation, although it does matter. Living a holy lifestyle will enhance our life on the earth both physically and spiritually. This is how we attain rewards in heaven (Revelation 22:12). Our holiness is based entirely upon our obedience to His Word.

> *As He who called you is holy, you also be holy in all your conduct, because it is written, "Be holy, for I am holy."*
>
> 1 PETER 1:15-16

3. *Three Groups of People*

> *Don't give offense to Jews or Gentiles or the church of God.*
>
> 1 CORINTHIANS 10:32 (NLT)

From the time Adam was taken out of the garden until the time of Abraham, there was only one group of people on the earth—the Gentiles. Out of the Gentiles, God called Abraham, Isaac, and Jacob and through Jacob (later named Israel), a second group of people was established by God. They were His chosen people, the Hebrews (Jews).

From the time of Abraham until the time of Jesus, there were two groups of people on the earth. One group was God's chosen people, His holy nation. The second group was every-one else. During this time in history, everyone on the earth was either a Jew or a Gentile.

When Jesus was crucified and resurrected, He immediately placed His blood on the mercy seat in heaven and took His place as the head of a "new" group. Everyone who believed in Him became a part of this new group. They were the Church. After receiving Jesus, no longer were they Jew or Gentile, but they became a part of His body, a new creation. Paul referred to this in 1 Corinthians 10:32 when he instructed his follow-ers to give no offense, either to the Jews, the Greeks (Gentiles), or to the Church of God.

As we stated earlier, all scripture is profitable for us as the Church, but not every scripture is specifically to the Church. To take a scripture that's written to Gentiles and apply it to the Church only brings confusion. Or to take scriptures that are written specifically to the Jews and try to apply it to the Church will cause error in one's understanding.

Without understanding that there are three groups of people on the earth today—the Jews, the Gentiles, and the Church—and without understanding that all three of the groups are addressed in the Bible, it is impossible to rightly divide the whole Word of God. In other words, the future of the Gentiles, the Jews, and the Church does not follow the same path into eternity. In determining your personal future, you must know to which group you belong.

4. *One Day is as a Thousand Years*

> *But, beloved, do not forget this one thing, that with the Lord one day is as a thousand years, and a thousand years as one day.*
>
> 2 PETER 3:8

In the beginning God created the heavens and the earth, and through the fall of Lucifer, the earth became formless and void (Genesis 1:2). Then through the six days of creation and a day of rest, God put everything back into order. These seven days are a template for the timeline of man on the earth. From the time that Adam was driven out of the garden until the birth of Jesus was approximately 4,000 years. From the time of Jesus until now is approximately 2,000 years. The six days of creation and the one day of rest represent the seven dispensations in the prophetic timeline of man, with each day representing a thousand years. With six days almost completed, the seventh day is very near!

In his letter, the Apostle Peter said that we should not forget this very important thing: "That with the Lord one day is as a thousand years, and a thousand years as one day" (2 Peter 3:8). We should not forget this because this truth is a foundational principle in understanding the "end of days." In Psalm 90:4, we are told that a thousand years in the sight of the Lord are like yesterday.

With this in mind, we can see that the six days of creation are equal to the 6,000 years that man has been on the earth from the time of Adam until now. And there will be a seventh "day," the day the Lord will rule and reign on this earth for one thousand years.

The Dispensation of Days:

Days of Chaos:

- Day 1—Light
- Day 2—Heaven

Days of the Law:

- Day 3—Land, Seas, Vegetation
- Day 4—Sun, Moon, Stars

Last Days:

- Day 5—Living Creatures of the Sea, Birds
- Day 6—Animals, Man and Woman

Millennium, Sabbath:

- Day 7—God Rested

In this six-day timeline, there are two days that are extremely relevant to the Church—Day 5 and Day 6. These two days, which represent the two thousand years between the time of Jesus' resurrection (when He placed His blood on the altar in heaven) and now, are called by many theologians "the age of grace" or the "Church age." The Bible calls this age the "last days."

God, who at various times and in various ways spoke in time past to the fathers by the prophets, has in these last days spoken to us by His Son, whom He has appointed heir of all things, through whom also He made the worlds.

Hebrews 1:1-2

We call it the Church age because these are the only two days (two thousand years) in all of human history that mankind can become a part of the Body of Christ, the Church.

We call it the age of grace because only during these two days can anyone be born again because of the works of Jesus instead of their own works. That's what grace is. God supplies the salvation; we receive it by grace through faith and it has nothing to do with what we have done. There is only one time in history this kind of salvation is possible and it's in the age of grace, the last days.

It is called the last days because these are the two last days before Jesus returns to set up His kingdom where He will rule and reign on His day, the Day of the Lord (the millennial reign).

The Year of Jubilee

(Leviticus 25)

In Genesis it states that man's days on the earth will be one hundred and twenty years (Genesis 6:3). While it is true that this is referring to the life span of an individual man of 120 natural years, it is also referring to the life span of mankind on the earth as being 120 Jubilee years. Let me explain.

The year of Jubilee is the 50th year. After seven periods of seven years each that equal 49 years (7 x 7 = 49), an additional year is added which is the fiftieth year, or the year of Jubilee (Leviticus 25:8-12). Many rabbis and prophets consider this fifty-year cycle as one year. If you count the number of Jubilee years from Adam until now (fifty Jubilee years) and multiply it by 120 (the years of man on the earth), it equals 6,000 years. This represents the six days of creation and the template of man's days on the earth. What a coincidence!

According to the Jews, man's days on the earth will be 120 Jubilee years which equal 6,000 natural years. In six days, God created the heavens and the earth and everything that is on the earth, including man. On the seventh day He rested. The Bible tells us that when Jesus returns, He is going to set up His kingdom, and in His kingdom He is going to rule on this earth for one thousand years, or one day. Corresponding to the seventh day that God rested, mankind is subject to the rule and reign of Jesus on the earth. We refer to this day as the millennium.

A Very Special Group

There is neither Jew nor Greek, there is neither slave nor free, there is neither male nor female; for you are all one in Christ Jesus.
GALATIANS 3:28

Remember that during Days 5 and 6 on the earth (the Church age), there are three groups of people. There are the Jews and the Gentiles and a group that was formed out of the two groups: the Church. This third group is special and unlike any other group in history. This group has the Holy Spirit living within them and for all eternity they will have special status with special abilities.

On the day of His resurrection, Jesus placed His blood on the altar in heaven. He became the once-and-for-all sacrifice for the salvation of mankind. The moment His blood, the perfect blood of the Lamb, touched the altar in heaven (that had never been touched by blood before), the Church came into existence!

From that moment on, anyone who confessed with their mouth that Jesus Christ was their Lord and believed in their heart that God had raised Him from the dead was saved. They became a new creation and they were no longer Jew nor Greek, but one in Christ.

> *Therefore, if anyone is in Christ, he is a new creation; old things have passed away; behold, all things have become new.*
>
> 2 CORINTHIANS 5:17

So, how does a person become a part of the Body of Christ? How does one become a Christian? Well, the answer to that is quite simple. According to the Bible in Romans 10:9-10, if a person believes in their heart that Jesus Christ is Lord and that God raised Him from the dead, and if they confess it, they will be saved—they will be a part of the Body of Christ. In other words, to become a Christian you must believe and confess. If you have never done that, right now would be a good time.

> *If you confess with your mouth the Lord Jesus and believe in your heart that God has raised Him from the dead, you will be saved. For with the heart one believes unto righteousness, and with the mouth confession is made unto salvation.*
>
> ROMANS 10:9-10

There are those who might be thinking, "It can't be that simple. It certainly can't be that easy to become born again or to become a part of the Body of Christ." However, let me remind you that during this time of grace called the last days, we are not saved by what we have done. We are saved by receiving what *He* has done for us (Ephesians 2:8).

The Church is a very unique group, like no other group in history. God's plan and design is for people to receive salvation based upon His grace instead of their own works or sacrifices. His plan for us to become joint heirs with Jesus and to rule and reign with Him out of the New Jerusalem in glorified, supernatural bodies is almost beyond comprehension. Until the Church is raptured, this opportunity is still available to all who will believe. But this special offer does have an expiration date! Don't let anything cause you to bypass this amazing opportunity!

Our Citizenship is in Heaven

For our citizenship is in heaven, from which we also eagerly wait for the Savior, the Lord Jesus Christ.

PHILIPPIANS 3:20

When a person becomes a Christian, as a part of the Church, there is a natural separation from the world that takes place because our spirit literally has the Holy Spirit living inside of us. Our thinking, our desires, and our understanding becomes different from that of the world. The more we saturate ourselves with the Word of God, the more dramatic that difference becomes. Because we believe Jesus is the Son of God and because we believe He is returning for us, our view on how to live our daily lives is different from that of the world.

As a young boy growing up in the Baptist Church, I remember singing the song, "This World is Not My Home." We sang this song regularly and I still remember the words: "This world is not my home, I'm just a-passing through. My treasures are laid up somewhere beyond the blue; the angels beckon me from heaven's open door, and I can't feel at home in this world anymore."

This song was written by Albert E. Brumley who lived in the early part of the 1900s. His words are so true. This world is not our home. As Christians, our citizenship is in heaven. When we receive Jesus as our Lord and Savior, our death is recorded on the cross. Old things pass away and all things become new. Our spirit becomes a born-again creation and this born-again spirit is born into the kingdom of God, no longer a citizen of earth, but now a citizen of heaven.

Although we are still living on the earth in our physical bodies, we are here as ambassadors representing Christ on the earth. But when we're caught up in the rapture and our glorification has taken place, we will be as He is (1 John 3:2) and our citizenship will be complete.

Now then, we are ambassadors for Christ, as though God were pleading through us: we implore you on Christ's behalf, be reconciled to God.

2 CORINTHIANS 5:20

As Albert E. Brumley said so well, this world is not our home, we're just passing through.

Expecting His Return

Looking for the blessed hope and glorious appearing of our great God and Savior Jesus Christ.

TITUS 2:13

As believers, we are led by the Spirit, whereas the world is led by the flesh. According to the prophecies hidden in the Word of God, as the time draws close for Jesus to return and gather His body unto Himself, it will become extremely evident who is waiting and expecting His return, and who is not. As the Church becomes more glorious and as excitement builds anticipating the return of our Lord, the enemy (who lives in the spirit realm) will also perceive that it's time for Jesus to return, and the social climate of the world will appear as raging insanity.

We must establish once and for all without question, without any doubt, the reality and the truth that Jesus will return as He promised. The rapture of the Church—which is Jesus coming to catch away the saints and take them to heaven (1 Thessalonians 4:15-17)—is the first of the two bookends on either side of the Great Tribulation. The second bookend on the other side of the Great Tribulation is the return of Jesus with the saints (the Second Coming) to touch down on the Mount of Olives in Jerusalem and set up His millennial kingdom on the earth (Matthew 24:30-31).

While the teaching of the return of Jesus in the air (the rapture) and His subsequent return to set up His kingdom (the Second Coming) may seem elementary and basic to students of the Word, it has been heavily debated, contested, and deliberated throughout the centuries. Lines have been drawn and often great division in the Church has occurred because of not rightly dividing the Word on this issue.

Remember, as you read the Bible, keep these four basic principles in mind and they will help you to rightly divide the Word of God. With a correct division of the Word, the prophetic scriptures about the return of Jesus and end-time events will become more easily understood.

Chapter Six

THE TIMELINE OF YOUR FUTURE

He has made everything beautiful in its time. Also, He has put eternity in their hearts, except that no one can find out the work that God does from beginning to end.

ECCLESIASTES 3:11

When we talk about heaven and the future events that will take place, it can seem very confusing. So, I would like to explain the future events for a born-again Christian. For people who have not received Jesus Christ as their Lord and Savior, the following timeline does not apply. So, in a very concise way, here is the chronological order of future events that will take place for the Body of Christ.

1. The rapture of the Church
2. The judgment seat of Christ

3. The marriage supper of the Lamb

4. Our return with Jesus at the Second Coming

5. Ruling and reigning with Jesus Christ during the millennium

6. Judging angels at the end of the millennium

7. Moving into our new eternal home in the New Jerusalem

1. The Rapture of the Church

All Christians living in this dispensation of time known as the age of grace (or the Church age) will enter into heaven in one of two ways. First, Christians who die before the rapture of the Church will have their spirits escorted to Paradise by angels. There they will live in their spirit bodies with memory and full senses, waiting for Jesus to return to the earth in the rapture.

These heavenly saints will return in their spirit bodies to the earth with Him at the rapture. Then their dead earthly bodies will resurrect from the earth and be caught up into the sky. Whether their bodies are neatly placed in a casket, scattered as ashes, or decayed into the earth will be irrelevant. The same power that raised Christ from the dead will quicken their mortal bodies. Their body will come together, regardless of its condition, and will be caught up into the air (Romans 8:11).

At that moment, the spirit of the departed saint will re-enter the resurrected earthly body and a great miracle will take place. In a moment, in the twinkling of an eye, corruption and mortality drop off the earthly body. The body is then no longer just a resurrected body, it becomes a resurrected, glorified body like the body Jesus had after His glorification, and which He will have for all eternity.

Those still alive when Jesus returns for the Church will not experience physical death but will be caught up *after* the dead in Christ are resurrected. The Bible does not give the amount of time between the resurrection of the dead and the catching away of those still alive. But when that moment comes, those who remain alive will be caught up in the air. Then together with all the Body of Christ, both the living and the dead will receive their glorified bodies at the same time.

Scripture best describes what glorified bodies will be like:

> *Listen, and I will tell you a divine mystery: not all of us will die, but we will all be transformed. It will happen in an instant—in the twinkling of His eye. For when the last trumpet is sounded, the dead will come back to life. We will be indestructible, and we will be transformed. For we will discard our mortal "clothes" and slip into a body that is imperishable. What is mortal now will be exchanged for immortality.*
>
> *And when that which is mortal puts on immortality, and what now decays is exchanged for what will never decay, then the Scripture will be fulfilled that says: Death is swallowed up by a triumphant*

victory! So death, tell me, where is your victory? Tell
me death, where is your sting?

1 Corinthians 15:51-55 (TPT)

Then all together the full Body of Christ, the Church, will go to heaven with Jesus!

2. The Judgment Seat of Christ

The first event for the Body of Christ after arriving together in heaven is the judgment seat of Christ. This judgment (Romans 14:10) is not to be confused with the great white throne judgment (Revelation 20:11). They are at different times with different groups of people. The great white throne judgment takes place at the end of the millennial reign of Christ, after the resurrection of the unrighteous dead. Its purpose is to bring final judgment on evil.

On the other hand, the judgment seat of Christ takes place *after* the rapture of the Church and those in attendance are the glorified saints of the Church.

For we must all appear before the judgment seat of
Christ, that each one may receive the things done in
the body, according to what he has done, whether good
or bad.

2 Corinthians 5:10

In Paul's letter to the Corinthians and in his letter to the saints in Rome, he told them that there would be a time when he himself, along with the Church, would stand at the judgment seat of Christ and be judged for what they had done—good or bad. The judgment seat of Christ will not be a judgment of salvation. Those attending this judgment will have already received eternal life and will be in heaven. This judgment will be where rewards are given based upon things done in the body on the earth.

> *But why do you judge your brother? Or why do you show contempt for your brother? For we shall all stand before the judgment seat of Christ.*
>
> ROMANS 14:10

Throughout the years, I have heard various Bible teachers say that the judgment seat of Christ is where Christians receive their reward of salvation, but this is not so. Our eternal salvation is not predicated upon what we have done, it is a gift from God established upon what Jesus has already done. It cannot be a reward for our good deeds. A reward by its very nature is a gift received for a job well done.

I've also heard people say that they do not need any rewards from Jesus. Just getting to heaven is enough for them. Trust me, if your Lord and Savior, who knows you better than you know yourself, has prepared a gift that is tailored specifically for you and no one else, you will be very thankful to receive it.

The grace of God is powerful. We are saved by grace through faith. But the grace of God does not determine our heavenly rewards. It is logical to think that if rewards are received as a result of good works, then there will be those in heaven with greater rewards than others. Understanding this reality should remove complacency and build incentive to be led by the Spirit.

There are many scriptures that verify that God wants to reward us for our good deeds. But what are the rewards? Are they tangible, spiritual, or are they a higher position in the kingdom of God? We are not told specifically what they are, but we do know that any gift from God is a good gift that you will desire (James 1:17).

> *Now he who plants and he who waters are one, and each one will receive his own reward according to his own labor.*
>
> 1 CORINTHIANS 3:8

> *But you, when you pray, go into your room, and when you have shut your door, pray to your Father who is in the secret place; and your Father who sees in secret will reward you openly.*
>
> MATTHEW 6:6

> *Therefore, do not cast away your confidence, which has great reward.*
>
> HEBREWS 10:35

> *Each one's work will become clear; for the Day will declare it, because it will be revealed by fire; and the fire will test each one's work, of what sort it is. If*

anyone's work which he has built on it endures, he will receive a reward.

1 CORINTHIANS 3:13-14

Look to yourselves, that we do not lose those things we worked for, but that we may receive a full reward.

2 JOHN 1:8

Recently, while discussing heavenly rewards with a young man, he asked me if it was true that once we become a Christian our spirit is cleansed of all sin and made righteous. He went on to quote the verse in 1 John 3:9 that states, "Whoever has been born of God does not sin, for His seed remains in him; and he cannot sin, because he has been born of God." He asked me if that scripture was true.

Of course God's Word is true! I told him all Scripture is inspired by God and is profitable. Then he proposed this question: if my spirit is cleansed of all sin and cannot sin, then why would I not receive the ultimate reward at the judgment seat of Christ?

The answer to his question is quite simple. We are not given rewards based on the condition of our spirit, but rather on what has been done in the body while living on the earth. His view of heaven would give everyone the same reward and equal status. It would be a type of entitlement or heavenly socialism. Since everyone's works in the body are not the same, this could never be.

This young man did not understand the difference between holiness and righteousness. It is true that when you become a Christian you are made righteous, your spirit is cleansed of all unrighteousness and cannot sin; it is sealed by the Holy Spirit until the day of redemption (Ephesians 4:30). However, your soul and your body have not been born again and are still susceptible to the temptations of the flesh. We become more holy as we become more obedient to the Word of God. Remember, our righteousness is a gift *from* God as a result of what Jesus has done for us. Our holiness is a gift *to* God from us as a result of what we have done.

> *Let no one cheat you of your reward, taking delight in false humility and worship of angels, intruding into those things which he has not seen, vainly puffed up by his fleshly mind.*
>
> COLOSSIANS 2:18

Everyone at the judgment seat of Christ will have already been made righteous and will be judged on the things done while in their physical bodies on the earth, whether good or bad. Jesus himself will hand out the rewards that He has prepared for us. This truth should be motivation to live a holy life in our remaining days on the earth.

> *Behold, I am coming quickly, and My reward is with Me, to give to every one according to his work.*
>
> REVELATION 22:12

3. The Marriage Supper of the Lamb

The Church is the Bride of Christ, and the judgment seat of Christ is the adorning of the bride in preparation of the marriage to the Bridegroom.

> *Husbands, love your wives, just as Christ also loved the Church and gave Himself for her, that He might sanctify and cleanse her with the washing of water by the word, that He might present her to Himself a glorious Church, not having spot or wrinkle or any such thing, but that she should be holy and without blemish.*
>
> EPHESIANS 5:25-27

In Paul's letter to the Ephesians, he clearly described the relationship between Christ and the Church. He said that husbands should love their wives in the same way that Christ loved the Church. The greatest love a person can have for another would be to demonstrate that love by sacrificing their life for them (John 15:13). That's exactly what Jesus did for the Church.

In the same way that an earthly marriage between a man and a woman marks the beginning of a covenant of unity, likewise, the marriage supper of the Lamb demonstrates the eternal unity between the Lord Jesus and His Church. The Church is currently joint heirs with Jesus (Romans 8:17), but at the wedding feast, the inheritance is received. This covenant relationship between Jesus and His Church authorizes us to move into the millennium and to rule and reign with Him. The marriage is complete.

> *Blessed be the God and Father of our Lord Jesus Christ, who according to His abundant mercy has begotten us again to a living hope through the resurrection of Jesus Christ from the dead, to an inheritance incorruptible and undefiled and that does not fade away, reserved in heaven for you.*
>
> 1 PETER 1:3-4

The Apostle John prophetically wrote that the marriage of the Lamb and His wife would be complete *before* Jesus comes to earth to set up His kingdom (Revelation 19:14).

> *Let us be glad and rejoice and give Him glory, for the marriage of the Lamb has come, and His wife has made herself ready. And to her it was granted to be arrayed in fine linen, clean and bright, for the fine linen is the righteous acts of the saints.*
>
> REVELATION 19:7-8

When Jesus was preparing His disciples for His upcoming departure in John 14, He inserted a picture of where He was going. He was going to His Father's house to prepare a place for them there. While He was gone, He would not leave them as orphans to struggle on earth but would send a Helper (the Holy Spirit) to be with them until He returned for them (John 14:16-18). Then He would take them to His Father's house so they would forever be with Him.

Let not your heart be troubled; you believe in God, believe also in Me. In My Father's house are many mansions; if it were not so, I would have told you. I go to prepare a place for you.

JOHN 14:1-2

This passage gives us an understanding that Jesus will be preparing a place for us in heaven. However, the disciples, being Jewish, had a much deeper understanding because they recognized that He was making reference to the customs in a Jewish wedding. Remember, Jesus was not talking to Americans or another modern culture, He was talking to first-century Jews.

Jewish Wedding Customs

The concept of the marriage supper of the Lamb becomes more understandable when we view it in terms of the Jewish wedding customs during the days of Jesus. Generally, the wedding had three major parts. First, a dowry would be paid to the bride or her family and a contract was agreed upon by the parents of the bride and the bridegroom. This action marked the start of the time of betrothal.

Today in western culture, it would correspond to the time of engagement. It was during this time of betrothal between Joseph and Mary that she was found to be with child (Luke 2:5).

The second part of the Jewish marriage custom occurred a year later. At that time, the bridegroom and his male friends would go to the house of the bride during the night.

The bride would know that he was coming, but she did not know the exact time of his arrival. In order for her to be taken to the bridegroom's house, she had to be ready when the bridegroom arrived. When he arrived, the bride and her party would follow the bridegroom and his men to the bridegroom's house.

The last phase is the marriage supper itself. The marriage supper and the celebration that followed usually lasted for seven days. Many people were invited to this time of celebration, but only the ones who accepted the invitation to the father's house were a part of the wedding celebration.

In the same way, when we receive Jesus as our Lord and Savior, it is a type of betrothal and we are to be ready, waiting, and looking forward to our Bridegroom's arrival (rapture). He will take us to His Father's house where the prayer of the Bridegroom in John 17 will be fulfilled. The Church will be united with Jesus and there will be a major celebration in Heaven. For one week (Daniel's 70th week) we will celebrate our union with Him in heaven.

> *Father, I desire that they also whom You gave Me may be with Me where I am, that they may behold My glory which You have given Me; for You loved Me before the foundation of the world.*
>
> JOHN 17:24

4. Our Return with Jesus at the Second Coming

Behold, He is coming with clouds, and every eye will see Him, even they who pierced Him. And all the tribes of the earth will mourn because of Him.

REVELATION 1:7

Jesus said that immediately after the tribulation, the sun would be darkened, the moon would not give off its light, stars would fall from heaven, and the powers of the heavens would be shaken. After that, He would send out His angels to gather His elect (that's us) from one end of heaven to the other (Matthew 24:29-31). Then the Son of Man would come back to the earth with great power and glory.

The Apostle John, in describing the vision he received while he was exiled on the Isle of Patmos, said that he saw heaven opened. There was a white horse and the one that sat on this horse was called Faithful and True. His eyes were like a flame of fire and on His head were many crowns. He was clothed in a robe dipped in blood and His name was called the Word of God. As He rode, the armies of heaven followed Him, and out of His mouth was a sharp sword with which He would strike the nations. And on His robe and on His thigh a name was written: "KING OF KINGS AND LORD OF LORDS" (Revelation 19:11-16).

Who were those following the King of Kings on white horses? Who was the army that came back to the earth with Him at the Second Coming? It's the glorified Church.

His wife has made herself ready. And to her it was granted to be arrayed in fine linen, clean and bright.

REVELATION 19:7-8

And the armies in heaven, clothed in fine linen, white and clean, followed Him on white horses.

REVELATION 19:14

The seven years of preparation in heaven, the rewards, the marriage supper, and the celebrations will have prepared the Body of Christ to return to the earth to rule and reign with Him for the following thousand years.

On the earth during the tribulation, the beast and the kings of the earth will gather to make war against the King of Kings. The false prophet, who works signs and wonders, and the beast will be captured and cast alive into the lake of fire. The rest of the armies will be killed with the sword that proceeds from the mouth of the King of Kings (Revelation 19:19-21).

With the beast and the false prophet cast into the lake of fire and the armies of the Antichrist defeated, an angel will come down from heaven and take hold of the dragon, the serpent of old, the one who we know as the Devil and Satan, and bind him and cast him into a bottomless pit which will be sealed for a thousand years. No longer will he deceive the nations (Revelation 20:2-3).

> *Yet you will be brought down to Sheol, to the lowest parts of the Pit. Those who see you will stare at you, reflecting on what has become of you: "Is this the one who shook the earth, who made kingdoms tremble, who made the world a wilderness and destroyed its cities, who never opened the house of his prisoners?"*
>
> ISAIAH 14:15-17 (TLV)

For the next thousand years, peace will be restored to the earth and the King of Kings and the Lord of Lords will be the Sovereign Ruler. Those who returned with Him, the glorified Church, will also rule for a thousand years. Some may ask, "Rule over whom?"

5. Ruling and Reigning with Jesus Christ During the Millennium

Human beings with flesh-and-blood bodies will be living on the earth during the millennial reign. This will include those who were living during the tribulation and did not take the mark of the beast but gave honor to the Lord. The righteous Jews that were resurrected into mortal bodies at the Second Coming will also be living on the earth in Israel.

And many of those who sleep in the dust of the earth shall awake, some to everlasting life, some to shame and everlasting contempt.
DANIEL 12:2

The lives of these flesh-and-blood humans will be extended, but the people living in the Gentile nations will need healing, which can only be obtained by their access to the leaves on the tree of life. Their access to the healing leaves will be determined by their honor toward Israel. This is where the prophecy receives its ultimate fulfillment—those who bless Israel will be blessed, and those who curse Israel will be cursed (Genesis 12:3).

But we, who are part of the Body of Christ, will not be in an earthly body. We will be living in a body like the one that the King of Kings and Lord of Lords has. It will be eternal and will never decay. We will be assisting Him as under-rulers over His kingdom throughout the millennium. The Holy Bible does not give great detail on the method of our rulership, but we know that without the influence of Satan on the earth, and with the knowledge that for all eternity we will be with our Savior, it will be more glorious than we could ever imagine!

All Christians in their glorified bodies will be part of the ruling class during the millennium. Ephesians 2:6 tells us we are seated with Christ. Nowhere in Scripture does it indicate that any other group of humans or angels will be seated with the Lord. The Church is referred to as kings and priests in Revelation 1:6, and in Revelation 5:10 we are told that we will reign on the earth. The Church will reign as the bride and as rulers with Him (2 Timothy 2:12).

> *But God ... made us alive together with Christ ... and raised us up together and made us sit together in the heavenly places in Christ Jesus.*
>
> EPHESIANS 2:4-6

> *To Him who loved us and washed us from our sins in His own blood, and has made us kings and priests to His God and Father, to Him be glory and dominion forever and ever. Amen.*
>
> REVELATION 1:5-6

> *For You were slain and have redeemed us to God by Your blood out of every tribe and tongue and people and nation, and have made us kings and priests to our God; and we shall reign on the earth.*
>
> REVELATION 5:9-10

In Revelation 20:4, the ones who were beheaded are tribulation saints and are not a part of the group seated on thrones. In the first sentence, you will note they are separated by the word *and* (Greek - *kai*) which signifies they are not the same group, but two different groups. The word *they* at the end of the verse is referring to the ones who sat upon the thrones.

> *And I saw thrones, and they sat upon them, and judgment was given unto them:* **and** *I saw the souls of them that were beheaded for the witness of Jesus, and for the word of God, and which had not worshipped the beast,*

*neither his image, neither had received his mark upon their foreheads, or in their hands; and **they** lived and reigned with Christ a thousand years.*

Revelation 20:4 (KJV)

6. Judging Angels at the End of the Millennium

As the millennium comes to a close, the Church will proclaim final judgment on the fallen angels. The angels who rebelled with Lucifer were cast to the earth with him. Some of these fallen angels committed further sin by mating with earthly women as described in Genesis 6. Those angels who sinned at the time of Noah were bound by chains in pits of darkness as described in 2 Peter 2:4. The ultimate judgment for the devil, and all of the angels who followed him, is eternal damnation in the lake of fire.

In Paul's letter to the Corinthians, he made a very interesting statement concerning one of the functions of the Church at the end of the millennium. When the fallen angels are judged and committed to eternal damnation with their leader, Satan, it will be the Church that pronounces judgment upon them.

Remember that the angels are created beings, and that Lucifer's original sin was wanting to be like God the Most High. But in his final judgment, he will be judged by another created being—man. Through the grace of God, man was created in the likeness and image of God, elevated to rulership, and given an eternal glorified body just like the Son of God. This is the ultimate humiliation for the prince of darkness and the fallen angels.

> *Do you not know that the saints will judge the*
> *world?... Do you not know that we shall judge angels?*
>
> 1 CORINTHIANS 6:2-3

7. Moving into our New Eternal Home in the New Jerusalem

In My Father's house are many mansions; if it were
not so, I would have told you. I go to prepare a place
for you.

> JOHN 14:2

When Jesus was gathered with His disciples on the eve of His crucifixion, He gave them deep insight into their eternal home. The response they gave to the conversation revealed that they didn't fully understand what He was saying, even though His message was quite profound (John 14:5,8). Jesus told His disciples He was going to depart to prepare an eternal home for them.

Shortly after His resurrection, these same disciples (except Judas) received Jesus as Lord, were filled with the Holy Spirit in the upper room and became apostles in the Body of Christ (the Church). One of these apostles, John, wrote the Revelation of Jesus Christ that clearly reveals the future of the saints of God and their dwelling place for all eternity.

It is difficult for us to imagine the magnificence of our future home, but we can be assured of these truths. As the New Jerusalem descends out of heaven as described in John's Revelation, all of creation will be in awe of its brilliance. There will be no temple and the glory of the Lamb will be its light. The entry gates and the interior of this new heavenly city are so vast and contain such beauty that it's easy to understand why Paul said there were no words that could be spoken that could adequately describe this wondrous sight. And he had not even seen the fullness of our heavenly home, he had merely seen Paradise.

Remember, Jesus said He was preparing a place for us. We should not forget that in the beginning, He was there. He was the spoken Word of God that created the universe and without Him, nothing was made that was made (John 1:3). When we consider the vastness and the beauty of the expanse that we can see, earthly words will never be able to express the vastness and the beauty of the expanse that we cannot see.

So, where will we be living throughout eternity? Paul summed it up in the following statement. For those of us who receive Jesus as Lord and Savior, we will forever be with Him.

> *Then we who are alive and remain shall be caught up together with them in the clouds to meet the Lord in the air. And thus, we shall always be with the Lord. Therefore comfort one another with these words.*
>
> 1 Thessalonians 4:17-18

Chapter Seven

PROOF OF
THE RAPTURE

*Wait for His Son from heaven, whom He raised from
the dead, even Jesus who delivers us from the wrath
to come.*

1 THESSALONIANS 1:10

The teaching of the rapture of the Church has been very controversial. There are those who strongly teach that the rapture is fictitious and only a recent revelation to those who are teaching it. They say the early Church fathers spoke nothing about a rapture and that, in fact, the word *rapture* does not appear even once in the Bible.

The Holy Scriptures are the ultimate truth, and with that in mind, let's examine what they say. Jesus said that if we would abide in His Word, we would know the truth and the truth would set us free (John 8:31-32).

The Bible teaches of a time of great tribulation that will take place on the earth. This tribulation will last seven years. During this time, the wrath of God will be poured out on the earth while Satan is attempting to take control through the beast and the false prophet. However, the Bible clearly tells us that the Church is not appointed to wrath. The wrath of God will not be poured out on the Church because the Church will be caught away before this time of tribulation.

> *For God did not appoint us to wrath, but to obtain salvation through our Lord Jesus Christ.*
>
> 1 THESSALONIANS 5:9

In the early Church, there was a strong teaching that Jesus was returning for them, but as time passed, some Christians died and the question came up, "When Jesus returns, what about those who have died?"

In addressing that question, Paul wrote to the Church in Thessalonica. He said, "Beloved brothers and sisters, we want you to be quite certain about the truth concerning those who have passed away, so that you won't be overwhelmed with grief like many others who have no hope. For if we believe that Jesus died and rose again, we also believe that God will bring with Jesus those who died while believing in him. This is the word of the Lord: we who are alive in Him and remain on earth when the Lord appears will by no means have an advantage over those who have already died, for both will rise together" (1 Thessalonians 4:13-15 TPT).

He told them that when the Lord descends from heaven, it will be no quiet event! "For the Lord Himself will appear with the declaration of victory, the shout of an archangel, and the trumpet blast of God. He will descend from the heavenly realm and command those who are dead in Christ to rise first. Then we who are alive will join them, transported together in clouds to have an encounter with the Lord in the air, and we will be forever joined with the Lord. So encourage one another with these truths" (1 Thessalonians 4:16-18 TPT).

Harpazo = Rapero = Rapture

For those who say the word "rapture" is not in the Bible, they are right. But as we said earlier, the word *trinity* is not in the Bible either. However, we know that the Father, the Son, and the Holy Spirit are one. The concept of the trinity clearly exists without the word *trinity* being used.

The word *rapture* comes from the translation of the Latin word *rapero* from the Vulgate Bible which was a late fourth-century translation of the Bible. We know that the original languages of the Bible are Hebrew in the Old Testament and Greek in the New Testament. The word *rapero* was translated from the original Greek word *harpazo*, which simply means to be caught up or snatched away. This is the word that is used in 1 Thessalonians 4:17. So, whether you use the word *rapture* or the phrases "caught up" or "snatched away," the meaning is the same. Jesus is coming back to catch up, snatch away, or we could even say *rapture*, the Church to heaven.

One Event—Four Stages

When the entire Body of Christ is gathered together for the first time in history, a supernatural miracle takes place. First, the spirits of those who have returned with Jesus are reunited with their resurrected bodies in the air. Next, the saints living on the earth are caught up in the air and both groups together make up the entire Bride of Christ, filling the skies! Can you picture it? As good as things are at that moment, the best is yet to come!

After that, all the bodies of all believers go through a process of becoming glorified. The corruptible body puts on incorruption. The mortal body puts on immortality. Death is swallowed up in victory. These glorified bodies will never die.

I find it very interesting that Paul, speaking by the knowledge of the Lord, made a very clear point that this gathering in the sky will take place in stages.

> Stage one: the bodies of dead believers are caught up into the air.
> Stage two: the remaining living believers are caught up into the air.
> Stage three: the bodies of both groups are glorified together.

Stage four: all of the Body of Christ ascends into heaven with Jesus.

Paul said when Jesus appears, the dead bodies of the believers will be resurrected from the grave, and then later, the believers remaining alive will join them in the air. Why would he tell us this? What difference does it make?

Most movies, commentaries, and books about the rapture have these events happening at the same time. Some only focus on Christians being caught up and completely ignore the spirit bodies coming down out of heaven with Jesus. But, once again, why would this be shown in the Scripture as different stages taking place at different moments of time?

First of all, when the dead in Christ rise out of the ground all over the earth, it will be an unsettling event for those seeing it take place; but the Christians who are still alive need not be shocked or in a state of panic when this happens. I believe this is why Paul did not want the Church to be ignorant of this event. When it takes place, the ones who are alive and remain will observe the appearing in the sky, they will hear the trumpet of God, and they will see dead bodies coming together from all over the earth ascending into the sky. With this forewarning by Paul, those remaining will be able to observe everything taking place with joy. What a glorious event it will be!

The second stage of the rapture will take place for those who are still alive. But interestingly, we are not told how much time takes place between these two stages. It may be a few minutes, or it may be longer. But either way, stage one happens in enough time before stage two that the Lord thought it important that we understand this, and that is why He instructed Paul to write about it.

Another wrong assumption about the rapture is that when Jesus appears, everyone will shoot into the air in a split second, like out of a catapult. But that's not how the Bible says it is going to happen. The twinkling of an eye referred to in First Corinthians 15:52 refers to the rate we shall all be changed, not the rate of ascension. Jesus was talking to His disciples when He ascended into heaven, and the Bible says He was *slowly* taken up into the clouds. While He was talking to them, He began to ascend and then, He was gone. They stood gazing into the sky watching Him until He was out of sight. Two angels who were standing by said, "In the same way He left, He is coming back" (Acts 1:9-11).

Stage three and stage four will be glorious as the entire Church is transformed into glorified bodies. Then the Church, complete and knit together as the glorified Body of Christ, ascends to heaven with Jesus. I believe Jesus is our example in many ways. The body He has is the kind of body we are one day going to have. But in the same way He ascended, I believe, is the way the entire Body of Christ is going to ascend in their glorified bodies into heaven.

Sealed for the Time of the End

We are in the end of days, during the time when the revelation of the prophecies of the return of Jesus are being fulfilled. The mysteries hidden from generations past are now becoming clear.

In my library are many reference books that are hundreds of years old. In these books, the end of days is often thought of as one event. Everything from the rapture of the Church to the "coming down" of the New Jerusalem was wrapped up as a mystery of the end times. But in these last days, as we are near the time of experiencing these events, it's as though seals are being opened and we can more clearly see the details of these end-time events.

I remember a revelation that came to me when I was traveling from my home state of Missouri through Kansas to a conference in Colorado Springs, Colorado. One can see great distances when traveling over flat land. Traveling at night, I remember looking down the road where I saw a tall tower with bright flashing lights several miles away. I wondered what this extremely tall, well-lit tower was. But as I drew closer, I realized it was not one tower, but two towers. The closer I got, the more I realized they were not even next to each other. They were on opposite sides of the highway and I eventually drove between them. What at a distance looked like one tower, was actually two separate towers. But I couldn't see this truth until I drew closer to it.

This somewhat illustrates the rapture and the Second Coming. Hundreds of years ago they may have seemed like the same event. But as we draw closer to the time these events will happen, we can see clearly that they are not one event, but two events separated by the tribulation. Truly some things have been sealed up for these last days.

> *"But you, Daniel, shut up the words, and seal the book until the time of the end; many shall run to and fro, and knowledge shall increase"*... *And he said, "Go your way, Daniel, for the words are closed up and sealed until the time of the end."*
>
> DANIEL 12:4,9

Escaping the Wrath to Come

Although Jesus said that no man would know the day or the hour when He would set up His kingdom at the end of the tribulation (Matthew 25:13), Paul indicated that the Church would have a "heads up" concerning the appearing of Jesus at the rapture. He said that the world would be in darkness concerning this event, but the Church would not be in darkness because it walks in the light. He went on to say the Church would escape the wrath to come, and that should bring us great comfort.

> *But you, brethren, are not in darkness, so that this Day should overtake you as a thief. You are all sons of*

light and sons of the day. We are not of the night nor of darkness.

1 THESSALONIANS 5:4-5

Although we do not know the exact day that Jesus will come to catch us away, Paul indicates that we will know the times and the seasons of His coming. Because we are taken away, the Church will escape the wrath to come. What is the wrath to come? It is the Lord pouring out His judgment on the earth during the Great Tribulation.

> *Then I heard a loud voice from the temple saying to the seven angels, "Go and pour out the bowls of the wrath of God on the earth."*

REVELATION 16:1

All of this should be great comfort to every born-again believer. We can rest in the knowledge that before the Antichrist attempts to set up his kingdom during the seven years of destruction on the earth, the Church will be taken away to a place of safety, not incurring the wrath to come.

The Bible tells us that after the rapture of the Church, the world will experience the greatest harvest of souls ever known (Revelation 7:9-10). No doubt, once people see that the gospel is actually true, and that the catching away of the Church really happened, they will then decide to be on the side of Christ. However, they won't be a part of the Church. When the rapture occurs, the Church age is over. They will live on earth but will not have the supernatural bodies and abilities of those who were born again before the rapture, nor will they escape the wrath that is coming to the earth.

The Glorious Church

As the return of Jesus for the Church approaches, the world will become darker and the Church will become brighter. In Paul's letter to the Ephesians, he described the condition of the Church as she is presented to her Bridegroom, Jesus. He said that she would be a glorious Church without spot or wrinkle or any other type of blemish. Then he went on to say that the Church would be holy and without any fault (Ephesians 5:27).

It is obvious that the world has been falling into perversion and ungodliness at a steady pace in this last generation. The darkness has reached such a depth of perversion that, to some, it has become a normal way of life.

But on the other hand, in these last days, the true Church is experiencing a rejuvenation and awakening so powerful that the separation between the darkness and the light can easily be seen by those who are of faith. The anticipation of the Bridegroom's return for His bride is strong within the spirits of the true believers, and the joy of knowing His return is imminent is bringing a desire for holiness.

In Luke 18:8 Jesus asked this question. He said, "When the Son of Man returns, will He really find faith on the earth?" And the answer is, yes! He will find faith in the glorious Church that is waiting for His return!

Chapter Eight

SIGNS OF THE END TIMES

But know this, that in the last days perilous times will come.

2 TIMOTHY 3:1

All biblical prophecies agree that the current generation is near the end of days and the return of Jesus the Messiah, who will purify the earth and set up His kingdom. These prophecies reflect the destiny of the Church and the world.

The Church is the group of people who have received Jesus Christ as Lord. The term *Church* also refers to the Body of Christ, and the Body of Christ is composed of Christians. The Church is also known as the Bride of Christ.

When we refer to the world, we are referring to the system of ungodly government and activities. When the Church is taken away in the rapture, only the world's system will remain.

In the World, Not of the World

To further clarify this point, the Bible clearly says that Christians are not of this world (John 18:36) and further, they are not to be conformed to the world (Romans 12:2). In other words, we should not imitate what the world does; we should be imitators of God (Ephesians 5:1).

Also, the Church is told that the world will hate them (1 John 3:13), but that they should not fear because the Head of the Church, Jesus, has already overcome the world (John 16:33).

At one time Christians were in the world, but when they received Jesus as Lord, He took them out of the world (John 15:19). The Church is told to not love the world or the things in it, because if they do, the love of the Father is not in them (1 John 2:15). Jesus made it very clear that the reason the Church is not of the world is because He is not of the world (John 17:16).

As Christians, our citizenship is not earthly, but heavenly (Philippians 3:20). James, the brother of Jesus, who was the pastor of the church in Jerusalem, wrote to his congregation and told them that if they wanted to be a friend of the world, they would be an enemy of God, and would actually be committing spiritual adultery (James 4:4).

John the Apostle said that we as believers are of God, but that the entire world lies under the control of the evil one (1 John 5:19). Jesus said that no one can serve two masters. He will either hate the one and love the other, or he will be devoted to one and despise the other (Matthew 6:24). Another time Jesus said that it was no wonder that His followers would be hated because the world hated Him first (John 15:18). But this good prophetic word from the Apostle John should encourage every believer. He said that the world is in the process of passing away along with all its desires; but in his prophecy he continues with this wonderful statement that whoever "does the will of God abides forever" (1 John 2:17).

From the Garden of Eden until today, Satan, the god of this world, has done everything he can to destroy the plan of God for mankind. God's chosen people who stand in faith, and the Church, have a glorious future throughout eternity. But the god of this world and his unholy system of government will forever be banished into the lake of fire. God's prophetic Word reveals that as these end-time events are ready to unfold (both within the Church and the world), there will be signs to show us He is coming.

Giving Heed to Deceiving Spirits

The Spirit expressly says that in latter times some will depart from the faith, giving heed to deceiving spirits and doctrines of demons.

1 TIMOTHY 4:1

Several years ago, I was asked to be the keynote speaker at a leadership conference of a major Christian denomination. It's interesting that the organizer of this meeting, upon hearing that a former Southern Baptist pastor would be speaking, made a phone call, took the resort shuttle to the local Baptist church, and borrowed a stack of pew Bibles. Evidently the ministers attending the ministers' conference did not bring Bibles, but knowing that I used Scripture in my teaching, he thought that Bibles might be necessary.

From an early age, I have always been intrigued by the prophetic scriptures of the last days. So that day, I walked the ministers through a presentation of scriptures that prophesied the return of Jesus. I felt that I detailed and presented the scriptures so clearly that there could be no doubt that His return was an established event that could soon take place.

This convention was at a resort hotel that overlooked a large lake. After my presentation, I walked out onto the balcony to observe the beautiful view. After a few moments, the bishop in his robe walked out and stood next to me. He told me he really enjoyed my presentation. That put a smile on my face! But then he continued by saying that although it was a good presentation, he knew that I knew Jesus had actually already returned, and that the Second Coming was in our past, not our future.

While I was standing there stunned, wondering if he was joking, he continued by stating that, of course, we knew that Jesus was ruling and reigning at this present time and that we were already in the time of the millennium. I was at a loss for words! I stood there as he walked away, and the prophetic words of the Scripture came alive where it says that in the last days there would be scoffers and those speaking fables.

> *Knowing this first: that scoffers will come in the last days, walking according to their own lusts.*
>
> 2 PETER 3:3

I never saw the bishop again, but in the years that have gone by, I've come to understand that many Christian leaders don't regard the Bible as the infallible Word of God. Because of that, they are drawn away by every wind of doctrine that blows by and sadly, they become the blind leading the blind—entire congregations being led away into false doctrine because the one leading has no knowledge of where he is going.

> *For the time will come when they will not endure sound doctrine, but according to their own desires, because they have itching ears, they will heap up for themselves teachers; and they will turn their ears away from the truth, and be turned aside to fables.*
>
> 2 TIMOTHY 4:3-4

> *They are blind leaders of the blind. And if the blind leads the blind, both will fall into a ditch.*
>
> MATTHEW 15:14

Most Missed the Mark

There are many Old Testament scriptures that point toward the time when the Messiah would appear on earth the first time.

And even though no man knew the day or the hour, there were obviously those who, through spiritual insight of the prophecies, understood God's timing. While the world was confused and seemed to know nothing of what was happening, the wise men traveled to give honor to the King of Kings. The Word of the Lord came to the prophets to be revealed in due time.

> *But you, Bethlehem Ephrathah, though you are little among the thousands of Judah, yet out of you shall come forth to Me the One to be Ruler in Israel, whose goings forth are from of old, from everlasting.*
>
> Micah 5:2

Obviously, the wise men (who traveled from afar to bring Him gifts), Simeon (who was told by the Holy Spirit he would see the Messiah before he died), Anna (the prophetess who served God in the temple day and night), and a few other people understood the Old Testament prophecies and were able to discern God's timing of the birth of Jesus. But most people missed it.

From the first century until now there have been those in the secular world who have claimed to know the date that the world would end, and in the religious world, there have been those who have claimed to know the date that Jesus would return. Obviously, they have all been wrong.

In the year 960, there was a German theologian named Bernard of Thuringia who, through his calculations, prophesied that the end of the world would take place in the year 992.

Pope Innocent III, who was born in 1161, was considered by his contemporaries to be one of the greatest canon lawyers of his day. He proclaimed that the Second Coming of Jesus would take place 660 years after the rise of Islam in the year 1287.

Michael Stifel was born in 1487. He was an Augustinian monk and mathematician who discovered logarithms. He calculated that the day of judgment would begin on October 19, 1533 at 8:00 A.M.

Another mathematician, Scottish born John Napier (1550—1617), was a well-known physicist, astronomer, and astrologer who developed the use of the decimal point in mathematics. He predicted that the world would come to an end in 1688 or 1700.

Cotton Mather was a prominent New England Puritan minister and a graduate of Harvard University. He predicted the year of Jesus' Second Coming to be 1697.

William Miller was a famous Baptist preacher of the nineteenth century who predicted that Jesus would return on October 22, 1844. That day became known as *The Great Disappointment*.

Edgar C. Whisenant was a NASA engineer and self-proclaimed student of the Bible. He predicted the rapture of the Church would occur sometime between September 11th and September 13th in the year 1988. He published two books. The first was *88 Reasons Why the Rapture Will Be in 1988*, and the second book was titled, *On Borrowed Time.* He sold 4.5 million copies of his first book, while giving away 300,000 copies to ministers throughout the United States. When his predictions failed to come to pass, he wrote more books on when the world would end, using the dates 1989, 1993, and 1994. Edgar Whisenant died in 2001.

Harold Camping spent millions of dollars on billboards across the United States claiming that judgment day would be on May 21, 2011.

There was much publicity in the secular world predicting that some catastrophic event would take place in the year 2012. Books were written and movies were made concerning the year that the Maya calendar ended. So great was the publicity that many preachers attempted to align the Maya calendar with biblical scripture. Needless to say, 2012 has come and gone, nothing changed, and the earth continues turning.

With all these predictions that proved to be false, many have become disillusioned and have given up, saying, "I've heard all my life that Jesus is coming back, but nothing has changed. So, what makes you think He's coming back soon?" It is interesting that people who say this don't realize that they are actually fulfilling Scripture.

> *Knowing this first: that scoffers will come in the last days, walking according to their own lusts, and saying, "Where is the promise of His coming? For since the*

*fathers fell asleep, all things continue as they were from
the beginning of creation."*

2 PETER 3:3-4

Everyone reading this book should be thankful that these
predictions did not come to pass. Otherwise, all of us would
have personally missed being in the age of the Church.

Raging Insanity

Over many decades of ministry and with deep study of the
Word, I have had many ministers, young and old alike, ask
me when I thought Jesus would return for the Church. I will
proclaim here what I have told them: I will not set a date, but
I can predict the times and the season of His return by simply
quoting the Word. That brings us to this question: what does
the Word of God, the Holy Scriptures, say about the conditions of the world and the Church that precede His coming?

The Apostle Paul gave us prophetic insight as to the times,
seasons, and conditions on the earth as the last days come to
a close. When he was writing to Timothy, he said, "But know
this, that in the last days perilous times will come" (2 Timothy
3:1). Then he went further and detailed what would charac-
terize these "last days."

He said, "For men will be lovers of themselves, lovers of
money, boasters, proud, blasphemers, disobedient to parents,
unthankful, unholy, unloving, unforgiving, slanderers, without

self-control, brutal, despisers of good, traitors, headstrong, haughty, lovers of pleasure rather than lovers of God, having a form of godliness but denying its power" (2 Timothy 3:2-5).

It is interesting that he started his description using one phrase that characterized all the behavior he further listed. He said in the last days there would be "perilous" times.

The original Greek word Paul used that is translated *perilous* is χαλεποι (chalepos). This word is only used one other place in the Bible. That is in Matthew 8:28 where we are given a description of the demon-possessed man who came out of the tombs when Jesus went to the country of the Gadarenes.

The Bible says this demon-possessed man ran naked through the tombs at night and terrorized the entire region. In fact, the people in the communities had tried to contain him by chaining and shackling him, but the shackles were no match for his tremendous strength. He simply broke the chains and continued wreaking havoc on the community.

By current English definitions, we could correctly say that the madman described in this passage was "ragingly insane."

With this in mind, remember that the word used to describe the demon-possessed man is the same word used to describe the condition of the world in the last days—or the end of days. Surely this is coming to pass now. The world is currently in a condition of "raging insanity." The prophecy is being fulfilled in our day.

Many things that were considered perverted, unbiblical, and against the law only a few years ago are not only legal today, but considered acceptable by parts of society. Anyone who speaks against these acts of perversion may be accused of hatefulness, and many times they suffer persecution. In these last days, the world is obviously suffering from "raging insanity."

Bible prophecy tells us that in the last days the people in the world will call evil good, and they will call good evil (Isaiah 5:20). We are seeing this every day. Who would have thought that same-sex marriage and the killing of babies would be acceptable in a Christian country? The secular entertainment world considers nudity, profanity, and public sexual expression as artistic and acceptable. Like the man of Gadara, much of the entertainment industry is running naked through the tombs and the world is buying tickets to watch it!

Is Bible prophecy being fulfilled? Are we living in the last days? The condition of the madman two thousand years ago has infected secular society as well as the secular church. The demons are restless because they know their time is at hand. Today, the demons have entered the pigs and they are running insanely toward destruction.

Removing Fear of the Great Tribulation

Through the centuries there have been many church leaders who have claimed to know who the Antichrist was. When Napoleon led his armies across Europe, it was proclaimed by many that he was the Antichrist. Within the last century, church leaders have proclaimed Adolph Hitler, Benito Mussolini, Josef Stalin, Vladimir Lenin, and Vladimir Putin as candidates for the Antichrist.

I have a book in my library that was written just a few decades ago that asks the question if Henry Kissinger was the Antichrist. Some past claims bordered on the ridiculous. I once read an article that said Ronald Wilson Reagan was the Antichrist because each of his three names had six letters, thus equating to the code 666. Obviously, all of these past claims were false.

But there are those who ask, "What about the Great Tribulation that is so prominently discussed in the Bible? What about the wars and rumors of wars, and the great famines and pestilence that is predicted in Matthew chapter 24?"

It is true that there will be a man who will stand on earth as the Antichrist, and there will be a time when he will be revealed. There will be wars and rumors of wars. There will be a time of great destruction and famine on the earth. But this cannot happen until after that which restrains him (the Church) is taken away in the rapture (2 Thessalonians 2:7) and kept in the safety of the Lord in heaven. These events prophesied in Matthew will take place before the Second Coming, but not before the rapture. Great tribulation is coming to the world, but the Church has nothing to fear.

Much more then, having now been justified by His blood, we shall be saved from wrath through Him.

ROMANS 5:9

Because of movies that depict the end of days and show the great horrors of the apocalypse, many Christians fear going through the tribulation. Sadly, much of this horror is also promoted by ministers who do not rightly divide the Word of God.

Much money has been made by companies selling "end-of-days survival kits" that include water and canned food. Some have even stored weapons with large quantities of ammunition to fight off those who would attempt to break in and steal their goods. This fear is based on the concept that the Church will not take the mark of the beast, and thus, will not be able to buy or sell goods during the Great Tribulation. This teaching is based on fear, tradition, and not understanding what the Scriptures say about the years preceding the return of Jesus.

Once again, fear can come from not understanding and not discerning who is being addressed in the Word of God. In Matthew 24, Jesus tells of many terrible things that are about to take place. Part of rightly dividing the Word is knowing who the speaker is talking to as well as the context of the conversation.

These Jewish disciples understood the prophecies of the Old Testament and were simply asking when Jesus as the Messiah would set up His kingdom. The answer to their question is this: Jesus will set up His millennial kingdom when He returns at the end of the seven-year tribulation period with the glorified Church. The things mentioned in Matthew 24—the wars, rumors of wars, and great famines—take place during the seven-year tribulation. However, the rapture of the Church takes place before that.

The Bible tells us the Church has not been appointed to wrath. While it is true that there will be seven years of great tribulation here on the earth, the Church will be in heaven in their glorified bodies taking care of business.

> *God didn't intend for us to suffer His wrath but rather to possess salvation through our Lord Jesus Christ. Jesus died for us so that, whether we are awake or asleep, we will live together with him.*
>
> 1 Thessalonians 5:9-10 (CEB)

Rightly Dividing Matthew 24

Let's address what Jesus said in Matthew chapter 24. Shortly before His crucifixion, as Jesus was leaving the temple with His disciples, He made a comment to them that not one stone of the temple would be left upon another. As they walked to the Mount of Olives, He sat down privately with His disciples. They asked Him what the signs would be for His coming and the end of the age.

Remember, His disciples were Jewish, and they were only asking Jesus when He was going to come into His kingdom.

The New Testament had not been written and the concept of the Church was not yet understood by them. In fact, it was not revealed until after the Church was born.

> *The mystery which has been hidden from ages and from generations, but now has been revealed to His saints.*
>
> COLOSSIANS 1:26

When the disciples asked Jesus about the signs that would be shown at the end of the age, they were not asking about the rapture of the Church. They were simply asking what the signs would be before Jesus set up His kingdom.

Although at that time the disciples did not fully understand what Jesus was prophesying to them about His kingdom, it was later brought to their remembrance and they received revelation through the Holy Spirit. But at this particular time, they did not even understand the questions they were asking.

> *Therefore, when He had risen from the dead, His disciples remembered that He had said this to them; and they believed the Scripture and the word which Jesus had said.*
>
> JOHN 2:22

Jesus told them of many signs that would occur before He set up His kingdom. He said that many would come in His name saying, "I am the Christ," and that many would become deceived. He said that there would be wars and rumors of wars.

He said that nation (ethnic groups) would rise against nation and kingdom against kingdom. There would be famines, pestilences, and earthquakes in various places, and all of this, He told them, would just be the beginning.

Then He went on to say that they would be hated by all nations, and that people would become offended, betraying and hating one another. There would be false prophets, many would be deceived, and love would grow cold.

Jesus was clearly talking about events that would take place during the Great Tribulation. These events occur before the Second Coming at the end of the tribulation and should not be seen as pre-rapture events.

Then He added this statement: "But he who endures to the end shall be saved." Those who endure and do not submit to the prophet and the beast during the tribulation will be saved from destruction if they endure. This does not make them part of the Church that has already been caught away by Jesus at the beginning of this Great Tribulation. Those who are saved from destruction during this time will enter into the millennial kingdom and populate the earth as humans.

Jesus continued speaking to His disciples saying, "This gospel of the Kingdom will be preached in all the world as a witness to all nations, and then the end will come." There are those who teach that the gospel must be preached to every corner of the world before Jesus can return for the Church in the rapture, but keep in mind, the rapture is not the end, it is the beginning of the end. The gospel will be preached to all the world before the end—before Jesus returns to set up His kingdom at the end of the seven-year tribulation. The Second Coming marks the end of man's days on the earth. That is the end referred to in Matthew 24:14.

A Summary

The message Jesus gave in Matthew 24 was to Jewish men and not to the Church. The only way that all the end-time prophetic scriptures seamlessly fit together is by understanding that Jesus is coming back for the Church. When the Church is in heaven experiencing the judgment seat of Christ and the marriage supper of the Lamb, the Great Tribulation takes place on earth.

The rapture of the Church is the resurrection and glorification of the born-again Church of God that takes place before the seven-year tribulation. At the end of the seven years, the saints of God return with Jesus to the earth. This is the Second Coming where He sets up His kingdom for the millennial reign.

At the Second Coming is the resurrection of the righteous Jews and those martyred for the gospel's sake during the tribulation. The resurrection of the righteous Jews and the martyrs is into *resurrected human* bodies. With this understanding, all scriptures regarding the signs of the end times seamlessly fit together.

Chapter Nine

OUR HEAVENLY BODIES

For the trumpet will sound, and the dead will be raised incorruptible, and we shall be changed. For this corruptible must put on incorruption, and this mortal must put on immortality.

1 CORINTHIANS 15:52-53

In a similar way that a caterpillar changes into a butterfly, there are changes that will take place to the body of a Christian until they reach their final eternal state, which will be a glorified body like Jesus has. There are three possible stages of existence for a Christian:

1. A human body (the physical body we received at birth)

2. A spirit body (the body of a Christian in Paradise waiting for the rapture)

3. A glorified body (the eternal body of a believer after the rapture)

The Human Body

At conception, life begins and the human body comes into existence. Throughout the centuries, the question has always been asked, "When does life begin?" There have been some who say life begins when a baby takes its first breath. There are others who say that life begins when the child has its first heartbeat.

The Word of God tells us that when a man and a woman come together, they become one flesh (Genesis 2:24; Mark 10:8). This coming together takes place when the sperm of a man enters the egg of a woman, and that ever-so-tiny burst of light takes place. Although the fully manifested creation is not complete, life has begun. The life of a plant does not begin when the stem breaks through the ground; it is when the seed germinates in the soil that life truly begins. In the same way, the life of a child begins in the unseen realm within the mother.

> *And it happened, when Elizabeth heard the greeting of Mary, that the babe leaped in her womb.*
>
> LUKE 1:41

> *Before I formed you in the womb I knew you; before you were born I sanctified you...*
>
> JEREMIAH 1:5

We remain in our physical bodies until one of two things happens.

1. Our physical body quits working and dies.
2. Jesus returns for the Church in the rapture.

Throughout our life on earth, our physical body continues to age whether we are a Christian or not. Even though our spirit has been born again, our body has not, so the aging process continues until the physical body dies.

An astronaut cannot be in space without a space suit. In order for the astronaut to live, the space suit must be functioning correctly. Likewise, our physical bodies are like earth suits. As long as it is functioning properly, our spirit can stay in it. But when our earth suit is destroyed, our spirit must leave.

The Apostle Paul said that when our spirit leaves our body, it becomes present with the Lord (2 Corinthians 5:8). The Bible tells us in Luke chapter 16 that angels are the ones who escort us to our eternal home. This glorious event should not be feared!

A Spirit Body After Death but Before the Rapture

Through the centuries, a teaching has periodically surfaced that says when a Christian dies, their spirit enters into a state called "soul sleep." Soul sleep is defined as a type of suspended animation where there is no consciousness until you are awakened at the return of Jesus.

There is absolutely no foundation for this teaching in the Word of God. In fact, quite the opposite is true! When a human being dies, their spirit either goes to Hades, or is escorted by angels into Paradise, both groups having full consciousness. Their thoughts and desires, their memory, as well as their senses are still intact with full awareness of where they are. We know this because of the account Jesus gave of the rich man and Lazarus in Luke chapter 16.

The ones going to Hades are in various torments and confined there until the resurrection of the unrighteous dead at the end of the millennial reign of Christ. On the other hand, the saints are alive and well in the presence of God, looking down from the cloud of witnesses on those who remain alive on the earth, cheering them on to victory!

> *Therefore we also, since we are surrounded by so great a cloud of witnesses...*
> HEBREWS 12:1

Much of the confusion concerning soul sleep comes from 1 Thessalonians 4:13 where it speaks of those who sleep in Jesus. The phrase "fallen asleep" is a euphemism for death. It's a phrase the early Christians used that described the departure of the spirit from the body that ended conscious existence on the earth.

*We are confident, yes, well pleased rather to be absent
from the body and to be present with the Lord.*

2 CORINTHIANS 5:8

*For I am hard-pressed between the two, having a
desire to depart and be with Christ, which is far better.*

PHILIPPIANS 1:23

Between the time you are living in a flesh-and-blood body
and the time you will be living in your glorified body, you will
be living in your spirit body in Paradise. In your spirit body you
will be recognizable to others, with full memory and communication abilities. With fullness of joy (Psalm 16:11), you will
be anticipating the rapture and your glorified body.

You Do Not Become an Angel

I have attended countless funerals where I've heard the minister imply that the departed person had become an angel in
God's choir in heaven. Nowhere in the Scriptures is this indicated; this is nothing but heresy.

Angels were created at a time before the creation of mankind. While angels can have the appearance of a person, they
are not human. They do not have blood and they are not candidates for salvation. When Jesus died on the cross, He died for
mankind only. Heavenly angels, fallen angels, heavenly hosts
and all other spiritual beings were excluded. The Bible tells
us that angels look on and have a desire to be human, but this

desire will never be fulfilled. Angels were created to be angels who will always remain angels throughout eternity.

> *To them it was revealed that, not to themselves, but to us they were ministering the things which now have been reported to you through those who have preached the gospel to you by the Holy Spirit sent from heaven— things which angels desire to look into.*
> 1 PETER 1:12

Likewise, men will never be angels. The Bible clearly says that man was created in the likeness and image of God. The born-again believer will eventually have a glorified body that they will retain throughout eternity.

We learn in Genesis that God's pattern is that every living thing reproduces after its own kind. A monkey never becomes an elephant, a giraffe never becomes a fish, and man never becomes an angel.

There is No Place Called Purgatory

There is a pagan teaching that dates back centuries before the birth of Jesus which claims that there is a place people go after death to suffer in order to be purified (or purged) of their sins. They say that through their suffering in this place and through gifts given to the high priests from remaining family members, the time in this place of cleansing can be shortened. Although this teaching has its roots in several pagan cultures, it was adopted and taught as a church doctrine. Because of this false teaching, many lost the true understanding of redemption.

> *And as it is appointed for men to die once, but after this the judgment.*
>
> HEBREWS 9:27

The truth is that purgatory does not exist. According to Scripture, a person's destiny after death is determined before death. When the body ceases to function, a person's spirit either goes to Hades or is escorted by angels into the presence of the Lord. Jesus clearly said that between the bosom of Abraham and Hades there was a great gulf that could not be crossed (Luke 16:26). There is no mention in the Scriptures of a place of purging before entrance into heaven.

To believe this teaching is to say that the work of Jesus was not enough, and that more work needs to be done. Believing in purgatory strongly implies that the suffering of Jesus was insufficient and that only by adding the suffering of the individual can payment be made in full for sin (Galatians 2:16).

Simply put, our eternal destiny is determined by our acceptance or rejection of Jesus Christ as Lord while we are living on the earth. Jesus said there is only one way to the Father and that was through Himself (John 14:6). Jesus paid the price in full, so any additional payment someone tries to make is useless. We are made righteous because of His blood sacrifice alone, and not by any sacrifice or purging that man can do.

In Him you also trusted, after you heard the word of truth, the gospel of your salvation; in whom also, having believed, you were sealed with the Holy Spirit of promise, who is the guarantee of our inheritance until the redemption of the purchased possession, to the praise of His glory.

Ephesians 1:13-14

Purgatory does not exist, and is a complete fabrication based in paganism.

For by grace you have been saved through faith, and that not of yourselves; it is the gift of God, not of works, lest anyone should boast.

Ephesians 2:8-9

A Glorified Body

On the day that Jesus was resurrected, an angel came and rolled away the stone from the tomb. I've often wondered why the stone needed to be rolled away in order for Jesus to leave the tomb. After all, during His forty days on the earth after His resurrection, He was able to travel at the speed of thought and to appear in rooms without opening the door. If this was possible, then why did the stone need to be rolled away?

I've heard people say that the stone was rolled away as a witness to those who did not believe. But I think there is a much deeper reality. When Jesus died on the cross, He died a physical death. Although Jesus is the Son of God, He came to earth as the Son of Man. He continually emphasized to His disciples that He was a man like they were. Throughout His life He was tempted, but He never sinned (Hebrews 4:15).

I've heard it said, "Of course, He didn't sin. He was the Son of God." And while it is true that He eternally is the Son of God, He came to earth as the Son of Man and was the first man to live a life completely without sin. Of course, He would not sin as the Son of God, and for Him to do so would prove nothing. But as the Son of Man, He proved that He could be the perfect sacrifice, the Lamb of God, without spot or blemish, to die for the sins of all mankind.

On the day of His resurrection, when God the Father raised Him from the dead, I believe He became a resurrected man in the same way Lazarus, the brother of Mary and Martha, was resurrected (John 11:43-44). Clearly, His resurrection was a miracle, but there was more to come. Standing outside the tomb, Mary Magdalene saw Him, but He looked to her like the gardener. In other words, He was not glowing or showing any signs of being anything other than a human being. But when she saw His face, recognized Him, and started to touch Him, Jesus immediately said to her, "Do not cling to Me, for I have not yet ascended to My Father; but go to My brethren and say to them, 'I am ascending to My Father and your Father, and to My God and your God'" (John 20:17).

Immediately Mary Magdalene went to tell the disciples that she had seen the Lord, telling them everything He had told her.

Later that same day, the disciples were hiding in a room with all the doors shut because they were afraid of the Jews. With the doors closed, Jesus physically appeared in the midst of them and said, "Peace be with you." After showing them His hands and His side, the disciples broke out with great joy. Then He breathed on them and said, "Receive the Holy Spirit," and He continued teaching His disciples (John 20:18-23).

Thomas, who was one of the original twelve disciples, was not with them the day Jesus appeared. It was too much for him to believe, so he told the other disciples, "Unless I see in His hands the print of the nails, and put my finger into the print of the nails, and put my hand into His side, I will not believe" (John 20:25).

Eight days later the disciples were in the same room and once again, the doors were closed and secured. But this time, Thomas was with them. Again, Jesus appeared and said, "Peace to you!" Then turning to Thomas, He said, "Reach your finger here, and look at My hands; and reach your hand here and put it into My side. Do not be unbelieving, but believing." And immediately Thomas believed (John 20:26-28).

I've always wondered why Jesus told Mary Magdalene that she could not touch Him, but then asked Thomas to touch Him? I believe it's because between these two events, He ascended into heaven on the day of His resurrection and put His perfect blood on the mercy seat (Hebrews 9:12). At that moment, He became the perfect sacrifice and His body became glorified.

He was no longer just resurrected from the dead; now He was resurrected and glorified.

So, what type of body does Jesus have now? According to Scripture, Jesus has a glorified body and will continue being glorified throughout all eternity. For the Christian, this is great news because the Bible says that we become as He is (1 John 3:2). In other words, we will have the same physical attributes in eternity that Jesus has.

We had a small glimpse of some of His capabilities while He was on the earth for the forty days after His glorification (Acts 1:3). He traveled at the speed of thought, appeared in locked rooms, and natural laws did not hinder Him. His body was not affected by material objects (John 20:19) or gravity (Acts 1:9). He was not a ghost (Luke 24:39), nor an angel, but a resurrected, glorified Son of Man who walked, communicated, and ate with the disciples (John 21:13-14).

The good news is this: If you have received Jesus Christ as your Lord and Savior, you will forever be like Him, living throughout eternity in a glorified body. That's something to be excited about!

Full Circle

With our glorified bodies, we can see God's plan for man coming full circle. Adam was created in His image and His likeness, and was covered with His glory. Adam sinned and the glory departed. God put His plan into motion and through His Son, made it possible for man to be redeemed and brought back into a glorious state. When we receive our glorified bodies, God's plan will have moved full circle, and our redemption will be complete.

On the sixth day, God created man. He said, "'Let Us make man in Our image, according to Our likeness; let them have dominion over the fish of the sea, over the birds of the air, and over the cattle, over all the earth and over every creeping thing that creeps on the earth.' So, God created man in His own image; in the image of God He created him; male and female He created them" (Genesis 1:26-27).

In this passage it is mentioned three times that man was created in the image of God. What does this mean to be "created in the likeness and the image of God"? Of course, we know that God is not a man—He is not human. He does not have flesh and blood. Jesus clearly said that God is Spirit (John 4:24), and Moses wrote in the Torah that God is not a man that He should lie (Numbers 23:19). So, once again, what does it mean that man was created in the likeness and image of God?

The word *image* indicates that man looked like God. Man was physically structured in a way that would reflect God's own appearance. It doesn't mean that man was made of the same substance, the same size, or even with the same abilities. But it does mean that man, in some way, resembled God.

The word *likeness* means that man was given the same will and desires that reveal themselves through actions. In other words, if he was like God, he would respond the way God would.

To give you an example, I have a son, and because he is my son, he has some physical resemblance to me. Some people tell me that we look alike. Likewise, my son's sense of humor is similar to mine. I'm not sure if that is a good thing, but that's what people tell us! In some ways my son looks like me and acts like me. You could say that he was made in my image and likeness.

That's what God wanted when He created man. His desire was for man to look and act like Him, to be in His image and His likeness.

So, we can see that in the beginning God's intention was for man to be like Him. But because man separated himself from God, it appeared that he was forever doomed to be downgraded into his own image and likeness, separated from God for eternity. But before the foundation of the world, God foreknew the decision that man would make, so He placed His plan into motion; a plan that would reconcile man back to God through Jesus (2 Corinthians 5:18). With this understanding, we can now realize why the Church (the reconciled ones) will eternally live in bodies that are in the image of Jesus after His resurrection and glorification.

In the beginning He created man in His likeness and image, and in the end, man will once again be in the likeness and image of Jesus. Remember, Jesus told His disciples that if they had seen Him, they had seen the Father, because He and the Father are one. God's plan is coming full circle.

It has been said that the Bible is the Story of the Glory. It is the story about how man was placed on the earth with the glory of God as his covering. When he sinned, the glory departed, and man was naked (Genesis 3:7). No matter how he tried to create a covering, nothing was sufficient, so death ruled. But God, with His plan, made a way for man to be restored to his previous glorious state.

From Glory to Glory

On the path to eternity, a Christian will pass through several stages of existence. While on earth, our born-again spirit lives in a physical body. After death, our spirit moves into the presence of the Lord, and at the rapture, we receive our glorified bodies. The Bible states it this way: we move from glory to glory.

We can all draw close to Him with the veil removed from our faces. And with no veil we all become like mirrors who brightly reflect the glory of the Lord Jesus. We are being transfigured into His very image as we move from one brighter level of glory to another. And

> *this glorious transfiguration comes from the Lord, who*
> *is the Spirit.*
>
> 2 CORINTHIANS 3:18 (TPT)

While our struggles here on earth before the rapture may seem difficult, we must never forget that every step forward for the believer is better than the previous step!

> *For I consider that the sufferings of this present time*
> *are not worthy to be compared with the glory which*
> *shall be revealed in us.*
>
> ROMANS 8:18

As we look forward, we have the blessed hope of always knowing that our best days are yet to come! God is a God of increase, so there's no reason why we shouldn't expect increase to continue in His kingdom. As we grow in the knowledge of Him, His kingdom, and His purpose for us, our joy and fulfillment will be forever expanding.

Chapter Ten

WHO IS IN HEAVEN?

But you have come to Mount Zion and to the city of the living God, the heavenly Jerusalem, to an innumerable company of angels, to the general assembly and church of the firstborn who are registered in heaven, to God the Judge of all, to the spirits of just men made perfect.

HEBREWS 12:22-23

From eternity past, God has always been a good God, full of grace and mercy, who has never changed. When we read scriptures that tell us that He is the same yesterday, today, and forever (Malachi 3:6; Hebrews 13:8), we understand that He has not changed from Old Testament times to New Testament times. But it goes beyond that.

God's ancient past is the same as His eternal future. He is a creator and He is love. He is compassionate and He is just. God is a good God and He has always been a good God. When He placed His throne in the ancient heavens on the sides of the north, His goodness flowed throughout His kingdom.

Lucifer was adorned with every precious stone—sardius, topaz, diamond, beryl, onyx, jasper, sapphire, turquoise, and emerald with gold (Ezekiel 28:13). Who adorned him? Did he adorn himself? Did he place himself as an anointed cherub in heaven? No, he did not. It was the good, loving God of the ancient past who adorned him and gave him this position.

All angels were originally designed to live in heaven, but when pride entered into Lucifer and iniquity was found within him, he, along with one-third of the angels of heaven who sinned with him, were cast down to the earth. He was stripped of his heavenly position, and the earth and the first heaven (the atmosphere) became his temporary prison.

> So the great dragon was cast out, that serpent of old, called the Devil and Satan, who deceives the whole world; he was cast to the earth, and his angels were cast out with him.
>
> REVELATION 12:9

When my daughter was very young, she asked me, "Daddy, why did God create the devil?" I'm sure that many have asked this same question. Although God created everything, He did not create the devil. He created Lucifer as a perfect being and Lucifer became the devil because of his own choice.

> *You were perfect in your ways from the day you were created, till iniquity was found in you.*
>
> Ezekiel 28:15

We must never forget that God is the one who exalted Lucifer and gave him great prominence in His kingdom, but it was ultimately the choice of Lucifer to rebel that caused him to fall and enter eternal damnation.

God's Habitation

Although God created the heavens and He can look down upon them as His creation, we also know that He inhabits heaven. Moses said, "Look down from your holy habitation, from heaven, and bless Your people Israel and the land which You have given us" (Deuteronomy 26:15).

It seems from this passage that upon creating the heavens, not only did He create a place for His creation, but He created a place for Himself. In fact, Jesus acknowledged that God was in heaven when He taught His disciples how to pray. He told them to pray by saying, "Our Father in heaven, hallowed be Your name" (Luke 11:2). Even though God created all the heavens that we can see, and even the heavens beyond our sight, according to the Bible, His habitation (the place where He lives) is in heaven.

The Angels of God

All the references in the Bible about God's other heavenly creations tell us that they are also in heaven. We are told that after the angels proclaimed the birth of Jesus to the shepherds, they went up into the heavens (Luke 2:15). And the angel that rolled away the stone (that sealed the tomb of Jesus), did so after he descended from heaven (Matthew 28:2).

> *Then I looked, and I heard the voice of many angels around the throne, the living creatures, and the elders; and the number of them was ten thousand times ten thousand, and thousands of thousands.*
>
> REVELATION 5:11

In the early days of creation, before the existence of man, God created angels in abundance. We know from Scripture that there are different classes and rankings of angels—such as archangel, cherubim, and seraphim—but they all have one thing in common. They are messengers of God that were created to worship Him and do His will. They have many attributes, but after man was placed on the earth, they were given the task of assisting and ministering for the saints of God. Paul the Apostle wrote that they were ministering spirits who were sent to minister for those who would inherit salvation (Hebrews 1:14).

While their home is in heaven, angels have the ability to travel back and forth between heaven and earth, in and out of the physical existence where we live. Their appearance can be majestic, or they can simply take on the appearance of a human being. They do not become human, but their appearance can be close to that of a natural man. Paul warned his followers that they should never treat strangers badly, because it was always possible that they were entertaining angels without knowing it.

Heavenly Angels Among Us

Do not forget to entertain strangers, for by so doing some have unwittingly entertained angels.

HEBREWS 13:2

When my children were young, we lived in a waterfront home at the Lake of the Ozarks. It was nice being able to go to work each day by boat. While having a beach in my front yard was wonderful for the children, getting to our house by road was quite a task! We had to drive on nearly eight miles of winding, gravel road before we could get to the highway, which was little more than a side road itself. There were no stop signs, no street names, just markers that were known to the local residents. One of these markers was a cup tree.

At one intersection about halfway to our house from the highway, there was a tree known as "the cup tree." The tree had coffee cups nailed to the trunk and hanging from the limbs. It was a large oak tree and probably had as many as a thousand coffee cups nailed to it, all put there by a local man. With its branches hanging over the road, it was an easy marker. When

I would give someone directions to get to our house by saying, "Turn right at the cup tree," the look on their face was unforgettable! We lived in a resort area, but the local hillbillies still ruled the back roads.

We had weekly Bible studies at our home, but each time a new person came, they would usually get lost on their way to our house. Several pastors attended our Bible studies, as well as nuns from the Catholic Church, along with a few hippies and church rebels. Our house would fill up once a week with praise and worship at the end of an eight-mile gravel road.

My wife's parents lived in Clinton, Missouri, which was a small rural town about eighty miles from my home. Once, while visiting my in-laws, I decided to give my wife some private time with her parents, so I went into this small town looking for something to do. I noticed a bowling alley and when I got inside, I found no one was there except for the person working at the counter.

So, I rented my shoes, picked out a bowling ball and went to lane one. After about fifteen minutes, I noticed that another person had come in. The bowling alley had eight lanes, and I was on lane one. The other person was on lane eight at the far end. For about an hour we bowled, and we finished at about the same time. As I turned in my rental shoes at the counter preparing to leave, he also turned in his shoes, so we struck up a conversation at the counter.

He looked like he was in his late twenties to early thirties. His clothing was casual, and he had long hair. He had a great personality and our conversation was very general. I remember telling my wife how weird it seemed at the bowling alley with only the two of us there. Something was unusual about this encounter, although at the time, I couldn't figure out what it was.

The next week at our home at the Lake, we were preparing for our weekly Bible study. I had just arrived home from the office and dinner was being prepared. As we sat down to eat, there was a knock at our front door. To my extreme amazement, the young man from the bowling alley stood there with his Bible! I had never given him directions, nor had I told him what town I lived in. There was no way he could have found our house, but there he was!

We invited him in, and he ate with us. He attended the Bible study, then he left, and we never saw him again. During the Bible study he entered into the discussion and gave some great insights. There was a peace about him that was indescribable. I am convinced he was an angel!

When Paul said that we should be watchful how we treat strangers because they could possibly be angels, that was not only true for his generation; it still applies to us today. If God's Word is true (and it is), there are heavenly angels among us.

Another example of angels passing in and out of our lives takes place when the Apostle Peter was in prison. His situation was perilous because Herod was about to bring him out for execution. Peter was such an important prisoner that he was bound with two chains and as he slept that night, a soldier stood on each side of him. In addition, guards were standing at the door guarding the prison so that Peter could not escape.

An angel appeared in the night and stood next to him. The area lit up and Peter, who was still asleep, was struck by the angel on his side. The angel raised him up and told him to get up quickly. Immediately his chains fell off. Then the angel instructed him to get dressed, put on his shoes, and to follow him.

The event was so surreal that Peter thought he was seeing a vision, but he wasn't. It was very real. He and the angel walked past the first and second guard posts unseen, and then the heavy iron gate opened by itself. After they went through the gate, the angel departed (Acts 12:5-10).

This is a perfect example of how an angel appeared and did things for Peter that he could not do for himself. But the things Peter could do, he was instructed to do on his own. Angels are ministering spirits sent to minister on our behalf, to deliver us from things we cannot deliver ourselves from. The angel that delivered Peter from his impending execution had the power to remove chains, blind the eyes of the guards, and open an iron gate without touching it.

Later, after Peter had come to his senses, he said, "Now I know for certain that the Lord has sent His angel, and has delivered me from the hand of Herod and from the expectation of the Jewish people" (Acts 12:11). It was true. The Lord had sent His angel. From where? Heaven!

Jacob saw angels ascending and descending out of heaven (Genesis 28:12). And while traveling with his family in a caravan to see his brother Esau, he encountered two camps of angels (Genesis 32:2) and he named the place Mahanaim (meaning two camps). The angels of God minister on the earth, but their home is in heaven.

Other Residents of Heaven

Before the crucifixion of Jesus, when Old Testament saints died, their spirits were escorted to the bosom of Abraham waiting for their resurrection at the Second Coming. They are now a part of the cloud of witnesses in Paradise.

> *And I say to you that many will come from east and west, and sit down with Abraham, Isaac, and Jacob in the kingdom of heaven.*
> MATTHEW 8:11

Not only are there Old Testament saints and angels in heaven, but there is also a group alluded to in Scripture called the heavenly host. Who are they and why are they called the heavenly host? It is because they are heavenly beings and heaven is their dwelling place. Beyond that, we are given little information on this group of heavenly beings.

There is great diversity in heaven. However, there is a pattern to God's creation that can be seen throughout the physical realm as well as in the spiritual realm. From the creatures in the depths of the seas to the birds of the air, the mammals and reptiles on the ground, the pattern of God's creation is evident. His creations in heaven are no less diversified.

There are several references to the seven Spirits before the throne, but very little information is given concerning them. However, they lend further credence to the diversity of the beings God has created which are in heaven.

The Apostle John wrote in the Book of Revelation that in his vision of heaven, he heard the voices of many angels around the throne. The living creatures and elders were there also (Revelation 7:11).

> *And the twenty-four elders and the four living creatures fell down and worshiped God who sat on the throne, saying, "Amen! Alleluia!"*
> REVELATION 19:4

The Four Living Creatures

The prophet Ezekiel saw a whirlwind coming down engulfed in a great cloud with raging fire. It radiated the color of amber from within the fire and out of it came four living creatures.

They had the appearance of a man; however, each one had four faces and four wings. Their legs were straight, and the soles of their feet sparkled like burnished bronze. Under their wings were hands like the hands of a man. Each creature had four faces: one was the face of a man; one was the face of a lion; one was the face of an ox; and the fourth was the face of an eagle. As they moved, they did not turn and as the living creatures ran back and forth, it looked like a flash of lightning (Ezekiel 1). Needless to say, these living beings were beyond description.

The four living creatures described by Ezekiel and the four living creatures that the Apostle John described in the book of Revelation are similar. They may not be the exact same beings, but they are definitely comparable and probably of the same order. These angels are an exalted order of angels whose primary purpose is worship (Revelation 19:4)

> *Before the throne there was a sea of glass, like crystal. And in the midst of the throne, and around the throne, were four living creatures full of eyes in front and in back. The first living creature was like a lion, the second living creature like a calf, the third living creature had a face like a man, and the fourth living creature was like a flying eagle. The four living creatures, each having six wings, were full of eyes around and within. And they do not rest day or night, saying: "Holy, holy, holy, Lord God Almighty, who was and is and is to come!"*
>
> REVELATION 4:6-8

When the Bible refers to living creatures in heaven, we can assume that there is great diversity simply from the ones described by the prophet Ezekiel. But with all this diversity, there is one thing in common: everything was created by the Word of God.

The Church of the Firstborn

Heaven is also the dwelling place of all the saints of God from earth who have physically died. They are absent from their physical bodies, but they are in the presence of the Lord with their spirit bodies.

When Paul was describing the heavenly Jerusalem, not only did he say that angels were there, but he said the general assembly and the Church of the firstborn who are registered in heaven were there also (Hebrews 12:22-23). That means all the departed saints of God who are the Church of God are in heaven with Him.

Paul said that we were surrounded by a cloud of witnesses who were cheering us on (Hebrews 12:1). Who is that cloud of witnesses? It's the departed saints in Paradise who are rejoicing with us and who are eagerly anticipating our reunion with them.

So, who is in heaven? Of course, God the Father and Son (Jesus), angels, heavenly hosts, living creatures, the elders, the Old Testament saints, and the Church. To say that this is all the inhabitants of heaven would be very shortsighted. We have been told very much, but there is so much more we have not been told!

But this one thing we know for sure: There will be a day and a time when you will know exactly who is in heaven because you will be there walking the streets and greeting the angels, exploring the vastness and magnificence of God's creation!

Chapter Eleven

HEAVENLY ENCOUNTERS

I know a man in Christ who fourteen years ago—
whether in the body I do not know, or whether out of
the body I do not know, God knows—such a one was
caught up to the third heaven.

2 CORINTHIANS 12:2

A few years ago, I taught a class at a Bible college on the subject of miracles, visions, and the supernatural, using illustrations from the Bible. Shortly after the class, I was approached by a student who asked the following question. "I believe the miracles you told us about are true, but why are they not happening today?"

As I pondered this question, I began to realize that most church-attending people believe the stories in the Bible but fail to understand that these same miracles can happen today. As we discussed earlier, the Church was formed on the day Jesus put His blood on the altar in heaven shortly after His resurrection and the Church age will continue until Jesus appears in the sky to take His Church to heaven to be His bride.

Everything that happens within this time framework that we call the Church age, is governed by the same rules. In other words, anything that happened in the life of any Christian at the beginning of the Church age can still happen to any Christian now. The same rules apply. Great men and women of the Bible who were New Covenant believers did not experience anything supernatural that cannot happen to a Christian today.

When you read about the great and unusual miracles that Peter and the disciples experienced, you should never view them as strictly biblical accounts that can never happen again. No, to the contrary! Any miracle that happened in the first-century Church can happen in the last-century Church.

With this in mind, I would like to give some examples from the Bible during the Church age and then testimonies from personal friends that I know well and trust. First, let's start with the examples of heavenly visions from the New Testament.

The Deacon Stephen

In the early Church, the apostles were overwhelmed with all the duties that needed to be done. Consequently, the decision was made to select seven men of good reputation, full of the Holy Spirit and wisdom to fulfill these duties. Stephen was the first one chosen. The disciples laid hands on these seven men and they became the original seven deacons.

Not only was Stephen the first deacon in the young Church, but he also became the first martyr. The Bible says that Stephen was full of faith and power, someone who did great wonders and signs among the people (Acts 6:8). Because of the great miracles, jealousy rose up among those who were in the group called the Synagogue of the Freedmen (Cyrenians, Alexandrians, and those from Cilicia and Asia). They debated with Stephen but were not able to resist the Spirit and wisdom by which he spoke. Because of their failure to openly prove him to be a false prophet, they secretly induced men to speak lies and stir up the people, the elders, and the scribes. When the tensions peaked, they came upon him, seized him, and took him to the council (Acts 6:9-12).

Upon arriving at the council to be judged, they had false witnesses stand and say, "This man does not cease to speak blasphemous words against this holy place and the law; for we have heard him say that this Jesus of Nazareth will destroy this place and change the customs which Moses delivered to us." Everyone who sat in the council, looked steadfastly at him and saw his face as the face of an angel (Acts 6:13-15).

Then Stephen stood and spoke powerfully to the council. He spoke truth, rebuking them. The Bible says when they heard these things they were cut to the heart, and they gnashed at him with their teeth (Acts 7:1-54).

Then a miraculous and wonderful event happened. Stephen, being full of the Holy Spirit, gazed into heaven and saw the glory of God, and Jesus standing at the right hand of the Father, and he said, "Look! I see the heavens opened and the Son of Man standing at the right hand of God!" (Acts 7:55-56).

Then they cried out with a loud voice, covered their ears, and they all ran at him, casting him out of the city, then they executed him (Acts 7:57-58).

The method of execution was stoning. Simply put, stoning is when the executioners pick up rocks and throw them at the person until they are dead. They stoned Stephen, and as his physical life was being taken from him, he called on God saying, "Lord Jesus, receive my spirit" (Acts 7:59).

"Then he knelt down and cried out with a loud voice, 'Lord, do not charge them with this sin.' And when he had said this, he fell asleep [physically died]" (Acts 7:60).

Several things are interesting about this account of Stephen. This is the first account of a Christian seeing into heaven. Not only did he see into heaven, but he saw Jesus standing at the right hand of God. It is also interesting to note that he saw the heavens open. There must have been some type of a veil removed or spiritual curtain pulled back. But whatever it was, there was an opening that God created for him to be able to see beyond this natural realm and into heaven.

Some people believe that for Stephen to see into heaven, his eyesight was improved to the point that he could see light years away. However, I believe that the distance to heaven is not measured by miles or light years, but it is actually another dimension close to this physical existence.

When vertical blinds on a window are closed, someone can be standing on the other side unseen. But with a small adjustment of the cord, the vertical blinds shift and make everything on the other side visible. Nothing on either side moved, there was just a shift in the partition that stood between them. There is a partition or veil between the physical world and the spiritual world, between earth and heaven, and when the Holy Spirit pulls the cord to the curtain, everything can be clearly seen.

Either way, Stephen saw the glory of God in heaven while in his earthly body. And remember this: Stephen lived in the same age of grace that you and I are living in now. Anything that happened to any Christian in the Bible after Jesus became the perfect sacrifice until the rapture of the Church, can happen to us!

They Covered Their Ears

Another interesting thing that occurred in the story of Stephen is that the religious leaders covered their ears when they heard the truth because it was hard for them to accept.

Once while in Israel, Loretta and I visited the Great Synagogue in Jerusalem for a Shabbat service. We are not Jews, but we respect the Jewish culture, and we love the land and the people of Israel. After all, the Bible says that those who bless Israel will be blessed and those who curse Israel will be cursed (Genesis 12:3). And I know that a blessing is better than a curse.

As we entered the service, I sat next to a very distinguished man who, when the service was over, introduced himself as the brother of the cantor that led the service that evening. It had been raining and as we stepped outside onto the porch, we noticed the rain had stopped. The street was wet, and with the streetlights in Jerusalem reflecting off the wet pavement, it looked like a scene from a movie.

As we began to depart, the distinguished gentleman who had been sitting next to me came over to us; he had his brother, the cantor of the Great Synagogue of Jerusalem, with him. After a brief introduction, the cantor looked at me and said, "You are not Jewish, are you?" I said I was a Christian, then he tilted his head and with a stern look on his face he asked, "If you are a Christian, why are you here?"

As I said earlier, I have a deep love for the land and the people of Israel. When I told him that, I will never forget his response. He very dramatically covered his ears, made a loud humming noise, then he ran down the street away from us. I looked at his brother (who lives in the United States, I later found out), and asked if I had said something wrong. He simply replied that it was extremely difficult for Jews to believe that a Christian would support Israel because of the Holocaust and the centuries of persecution under the sign of the cross.

So, it appears that the tradition remains to this day among some Jewish religious leaders. When they hear something that is hard for them to believe, like in the case of Stephen, they cover their ears and take action.

The Apostle Paul

Another interesting point about the stoning of Stephen is that the men carrying out the stoning laid down their clothes at the feet of a young man named Saul (Acts 22:20) who just happens to be another Christian who saw into heaven while in his earthly body.

Before he was Paul the Apostle, Paul was known as Saul the Pharisee. As Saul, he "breathed threats and murder against the disciples of the Lord." He was traveling to Damascus actively looking for believers that lived there. He intended to bind them and take them back to Jerusalem for punishment (Acts 9:1-2).

While on his journey to Damascus, a bright light shone out of heaven, and Jesus spoke to him, causing him to experience a miraculous conversion. That same relentless determination he used to try to destroy the Church, he now used to build the

Church. With fearless boldness he preached the gospel of Jesus and under the anointing of the Holy Spirit, he penned half of the New Testament.

Years later, he told of an experience he had of being caught up into the third heaven. He said this had happened fourteen years earlier, referring to an event that took place in Lystra. While preaching the gospel there, Jews from Antioch and Iconium had followed Paul there to stir up the people against him. The crowd became so angry that they stoned him and dragged his body outside the city walls to decay, believing him to be dead (Acts 14:19). However, the disciples later gathered around him and he got up and continued preaching the Word (Acts 14:20).

I've heard it taught that the people of the city were mistaken and that he was actually just unconscious, so when they dragged him out of the city, he regained consciousness and recovered. Personally, I believe he was actually stoned to death and his friends did exactly what Jesus said they would do as the Church: they would lay hands on the sick and they would recover (Mark 16:18), and they would raise the dead (Matthew 10:8).

Fourteen years after he was stoned, he recounted that he had actually entered the third heaven. It was so surreal that he didn't know if he went there in his body or out of his body. But this he did know—he went to heaven (Paradise) and heard things that he was not allowed to repeat (2 Corinthians 12:4).

The total understanding of what Paul experienced is beyond earthly description.

A Manifestation of the Glory

My background is Baptist. I became a Christian at the age of seven, was baptized at twelve, and from an early age I knew I was called to be in the ministry. I attended a Baptist college and shortly thereafter, became the pastor of a Southern Baptist church.

I always felt there was more to being a Christian than just going to church and trying to be good. My prayer was always this: "God, if there's more, I want it. If there are miracles, healings, or anything supernatural, I don't want to just hear about it, I want to experience it!" Those may not have been my exact words, but they were the essence of what I prayed daily. I discovered that when you ask God for something that is His will, He gives it to you (1 John 5:14-15), and it was His will that I experience more! Through a fascinating series of events that would take more than this book to tell, my college professor from Southwest Baptist College laid hands on me and I was filled with the Holy Spirit.

My life changed dramatically. I became a traveling speaker for Full Gospel Business Men's Fellowship International (FGBMFI). I was billed as the Southern

Baptist pastor who got filled with the Holy Spirit. During this time of ministry, I saw many great miracles and healings and I experienced supernatural manifestations myself.

One such manifestation occurred on November 2, 1991. I spoke at a FGBMFI convention in Springfield, Illinois. That night after the meeting, I woke up at 2:00 A.M. in my hotel room and hovering above my body was a flat sheet of light. It was about six feet long, two feet wide, and about three or four inches thick. This was not a smoky, fuzzy late-night dream, but a wide-awake vision. The edges of the light were sharp and crisp. It was as though a panel of light was hovering two feet above me. The rest of the room was dark. The light did not illuminate the room, but the panel was pure light.

I cleared my eyes and laid there for a minute or two, wondering what I was seeing. When I decided to touch the light, I raised my hand slowly and moved it toward the panel of light. My hand went into the light with no apparent physical effect. The panel was clear so I could see my hand moving into the light, through it, and out the top side. I slowly pulled my hand back.

I tried to imagine what it would look like to someone walking into the room. It probably would have looked like a clear piece of glass (with some type of lighting inside) shaped like a panel door (without a doorknob) that hovered over me. After waiting a few minutes, I thought to myself, "What can this be?" I heard a voice from inside say, "This is My glory!" I knew then I was seeing a manifestation of the glory of God.

That night was just one of many occurrences when God showed me that His miraculous, supernatural manifestations were not restricted to the early Church, but were also meant for the end-time Church. Jesus told His disciples that the same works that He did, His followers would do also. Then He went on to say that not only would they do the same works, but they would do greater works than He did (John 14:12).

Faith for Unusual Miracles

The world is a mess and in need of the miraculous power of God flowing from the Church. But sadly, much of the Church believes that the days of miracles have passed. In my early years of ministry, I had a professor at a Christian school tell my class that the miracles that occurred during the early days of the Church (in the Bible) were for the "transitional period." I have searched the Scriptures and have never found any place where the Bible refers to a "transitional period." It's actually quite the opposite. The Bible teaches that in the end of days visions and dreams will become more prevalent (Acts 2:16-21).

With this in mind, we must ask ourselves another question: Why are we not seeing miracles today on a regular basis? The answer is quite simple. All the promises of God are conditional and based upon faith. Faith is the catalyst that activates the power of God. Faith in its very simplest form can be defined as "believing God." Why do we not see the miracles today we should be seeing? Once again, it's simply because we only receive what we believe, and much of the Church believes that the age of miracles has passed.

But there is a remnant of people in the Church who are standing on the Word of God and believing His promises. They believe that the gifts of the Holy Spirit are for today. They believe that dreams and visions are for today and that the same things that happened to the Apostle Paul in the early days of the Church can happen today. Remember, the Bible says that many unusual miracles happened at the hands of Paul (Acts 19:11). What is an unusual miracle? It is something that doesn't happen the way you think it should or could happen. We must believe in order to receive.

Through the years, I have met many great men and women of God who have received miraculous manifestations in their lives. As an author, I have always been hesitant to quote or repeat testimonials from individuals. The reason, of course, is because I know the Word of God is true and I know my word is true. But for me to put my name to someone else's story is something I have always approached with great caution. However, I would like to share three accounts that are from trusted sources.

Dr. Gary Wood

Dr. Gary Wood has been a longtime friend of mine and has proven trustworthy in all areas of his life. I've known his family and I've seen the fruit of his ministry. The testimony of his automobile accident, his death, his vision of heaven, and his return to physical life are an inspiration. Gary lived a full life of character and integrity and now lives in heaven. I feel confident in the account he shared with me before his passing.

Gary Lynn Dobbins was born on March 1, 1949 in Dallas, Texas. His mother and father were both alcoholics and extremely abusive to him and to his sister. Gary had been sexually abused by his father repeatedly and throughout his life, he carried marks on his legs where his father had extinguished his cigarettes. As small children, he and his sister were left on the porch steps of his maternal grandparents. They were loving Christians who raised them, so he took on their name. He became Gary Lynn Wood.

They attended Hillcrest Baptist Church where Gary received Jesus Christ as his personal Lord and Savior. As he entered high school, he could feel the call of God upon his life as he sang praises to the Lord. He won the title of "Outstanding Soloist" in the state of New Mexico and it seemed like his life was on the path of a glorious future in ministry.

In 1966, he entered Wayland Baptist College as a freshman. While home from college for Christmas break, Gary and his sister were on their way home after visiting friends. They were in his grandfather's car singing "Silent Night" when suddenly there was an explosion.

Gary tells that a sharp pain seared across his face. A brilliant light engulfed him and instantly he was free from all pain. He slipped out of his body much like slipping out of his clothing.

In a moment, he was above the car where he could see his body as though the top of the car had been removed. He could hear his sister crying and as he looked down at his own body, he saw his life go by in an instant.

There was no fear, no sorrow, and no confusion. It was as though he was in a swirling funnel-shaped cloud that grew brighter and brighter as he began to ascend through a tunnel of light. He had a very tranquil feeling, effortlessly moving like the moving sidewalks in an airport.

Gary's Experience in Heaven

Gary told me that he could hear angels singing all around him, and he told me that he could specifically remember the words to their song: "Worthy is the Lamb that was slain to receive glory, power, wisdom, and dominion be Thine forever, O Lord, amen and amen."

As he reached what seemed to be his destination, he began walking on a lush, green carpet of grass covering a hillside.

When he looked down, he noticed that the grass came all the way up through his feet. There was no indentation in the grass where he had walked!

As he looked around, he saw the outer portion of a magnificent city. As he approached, there was a beautiful gate in front of him that he described as being made of what looked like solid pearl, studded with sapphires, rubies, diamonds, and many other precious gems. It was the most magnificent work of art that he had ever seen. The wall was so high that it seemed like it would go on forever.

At this gate stood a giant angel holding a sword. He was at least forty feet tall. His hair looked like spun gold, with rays of dazzling soft light flowing from this magnificent being. Another angel came through the gate who was checking the pages of a book he was carrying. He then nodded to the giant angel confirming that Gary could enter the city.

Suddenly, Gary's best friend, who had been tragically killed earlier, stood before him. His friend was to become his guide inside the heavenly city. His friend took him to a very large building that looked like a library. The walls were solid gold, sparkling with a dazzling display of light that loomed up high to a crystal dome ceiling. There were hundreds upon hundreds of books in this library. Each book had a cover of beautifully carved gold with a single letter of the alphabet engraved on the outside. Many angels were present, reading the contents of the books.

Gary asked his friend why the angels were reading the books. He explained that these books contained the records of every person's life who had ever been born throughout history. Everything that was done on earth, good or bad, was recorded in these books.

Gary watched as an angel opened one of the books and with a cloth, wiped the pages. As he did this, the writing vanished and the page turned red, leaving only a name. When Gary asked what that meant, his guide said, "The red represents cleansing from the blood of Jesus, your Savior, and the names were transferred to the Lamb's Book of Life and the sins were remembered no more." The guide then pulled a book from one of the shelves with Gary's initials on the outside. It was the Lamb's Book of Life. He laid it open on the table and found Gary's name recorded in the book. Next to his name were these words, "Paid in full by the precious, red blood of Jesus."

After leaving the library, Gary was taken to a grand auditorium. Everyone there was clothed in glowing robes and upon entering, Gary noticed that he was also clothed in a robe. He looked up and saw a beautiful spiral staircase winding up into the heights of the atmosphere. In front of him was flowing a beautiful, crystal clear river of water. Following the river with his eyes, he saw that it was flowing from the throne of God. Around the throne were twenty-four elders with crowns on their heads, with a beautiful rainbow of colors encircling the throne.

His guide then led him into the water. Stepping in, he discovered that it was only ankle deep, but then it began to rise until it covered his entire being and he was submerged. He could easily reach down and pick up golden nuggets larger than his fist. Diamonds and other precious jewels flowed through his fingers with colors beyond his ability to describe. It reminded me of Paul's visit to Paradise, where he said that his experience was beyond the power of a man to put into words.

Gary could communicate with his friend, who was his guide, without saying anything verbally. When he thought something, his friend knew what he was thinking.

Growing along the crystal river were orchards of fruit-bearing trees. Each fruit was a gift and when the fruit was eaten, the gift would explode inside of the person eating it. The fruit represented gifts of knowledge. Then he saw the tree of life which was gold with long limbs also covered with fruit.

There was a multitude of people singing. They were from every tribe, nationality, and color. They were singing, "All hail the power of Jesus' name, let angels prostrate fall." Being raised a Baptist, Gary asked his guide, "Why were they singing from the Baptist hymnal?" and he replied, "Gary, all songs of the spirit originate here in heaven, then they are given to someone on earth who will then birth that song into existence." Gary told me that years later, he heard songs being sung on earth that he had originally heard in heaven years before. Two of the songs were "Alleluia" and "He Is Lord."

Gary was then led to what looked like a school playground area, and he marveled at the brilliant colors of the flowers. No two flowers were alike, and he experienced sheer amazement and delight when he heard the melody of praise being sung by the flowers.

Then Jesus arrived and the children ran toward Him, to sit and listen as He ministered to them. There were all sorts of animals with the children. Gary wanted to talk with Jesus and his guide told him he would, but first there were other things he must be shown.

He walked on the transparent gold streets of the city and saw the brilliance of Jesus, the Son, shining on them. The streets were crystal clear, yet they were pure gold. He saw angels, so many angels, doing so many different tasks, but always praising God.

I cannot completely describe everything Gary saw in heaven, but one thing that impressed me greatly was when he described a large storage room filled with healings for people on earth. He called it a "spare parts room," and when people on earth needed a miracle, upon their request an angel was dispatched to deliver that miracle to the believer in need. But sadly, after being dispatched, some angels returned with the "spare part" because of the doubt and unbelief that was spoken from the mouth of the petitioner. When God makes a promise, we must believe His Word and all our words and actions must align with that belief.

Gary was taken through gates that sparkled with precious stones where he saw the place that would be his home for all eternity. No two homes were alike, and Jesus was preparing them for each of us individually. His friend dipped his hand into one of the buckets sitting nearby and flung the substance against the wall. Instantly, a beautiful floral arrangement appeared on that wall. Gary was told that his dwelling was not ready for occupancy yet, so he needed to leave.

Then the Lord Jesus stood before him. Gary has related this story many times through the years, but he has never been able to find adequate words to express what being in the divine presence of the Lord Jesus is like. But some things he shared about Jesus were as follows.

"He looked at me with the bluest eyes I have ever seen. I fell like a dead man before his feet, which shown as fine polished brass. He reached a nail-scarred hand out to me and lifted me up. He then lifted me into His arms and held me to His chest as if I were a little child. I felt the most wonderful, joyful, peaceful, powerful love that I have ever experienced. His hair and beard were as white as snow. He wore a regal robe of righteousness with a beautiful purple sash that said, 'King of Kings and Lord of Lords' with a belt of solid gold around His waist."

Gary said he saw indentations etched across His brow and forehead from the crown of thorns that had been placed there. No words can be spoken that truly describe Him. Gary said he wanted to just sit at His feet, looking into those compassionate eyes and worship Him through all eternity.

Jesus spoke to Gary and said, "There is a song for you to sing, a missionary journey you are to take, and a book you are to write. There is a purpose for you being here in this life." Jesus looked at him directly with His piercing blue eyes and said, "Don't ever buy the condemnation of the devil that says you are unworthy. You are worthy. You have been redeemed by the blood of the Lamb." Then Jesus said, "Why do My people not believe in Me? Why do My people reject me? Why do they not walk in My commandments?"

He told Gary there would be three things that would mark the time before His return: a spirit of restoration, a spirit of prayer, and an outburst of miracles. Jesus told him, "Remember what I tell you, for the Father and I are one. When I speak, the Father has spoken. Above all else, love one another and always be forgiving toward each other."

She's Using That Name

Back on earth, Gary was pronounced dead at the scene of the accident. Gary's sister, Sue, was praying in the name of Jesus for her brother. His guide in heaven looked at him and said, "You have to go back! She's using that name!" Gary recounts how he did not want to go back. He wanted to stay with Jesus, but Jesus told him, "You must tell the people of the world to get ready, that I am coming back soon!"

Immediately, he was shot out of heaven and hurled back into his body. Twenty minutes after being pronounced dead, the paramedics noticed signs of life and rushed him to the hospital. From the impact of the steering wheel, his jaw was broken in three places and most of his teeth were reduced to powder. The impact of the steering mechanism also crushed his larynx, which caused his death from suffocation.

The next day, Christmas Eve 1966, he woke up in a hospital bed with his head wrapped up like a mummy. He was told by the doctors that without a larynx he would never talk, much less ever be able to sing again. But the miracle power of God was at work in Gary's life. He became a great minister and singer for the kingdom of God for many more decades to come!

Branden Brim

The next account I would like to share is from a young minister, Branden Brim. I have known him since he was a small child. I'm very close with his family and I have seen him extensively when he was not behind the pulpit. We have even traveled to Israel together and other destinations, so I can attest to his faithfulness and sincerity. This account of his vision of a visit to heaven is in Branden's own words. Whether in the body or out of the body, just like Paul, we do not know, but what I do know is this: his account is genuine. The following is Branden's account of his heavenly vision.

"I had a cry in my heart for courage and God answered me through a vision of heaven.

"One afternoon I was lying on my couch worshiping God with my eyes closed when I felt a strong presence of the anointing of God. I began to feel something very hot on my chest and when I opened my eyes, I saw two angels. One angel was looking straight at me and the other was standing to the side, holding what appeared to be a stack of papers. The first angel smiled as he took a piece of paper from the stack and laid it on my chest. The paper formed itself to my chest, then went inside of me.

"I was then taken upward to a place which I knew was heaven. It was so bright! I knew it was not a dream. I felt a freedom in my mind like I've never experienced before.

"I walked into a classroom where there were forty to fifty people. There was only one available seat left and it was in the front and the center, so I took my seat (everyone else was already seated). I looked around and behind me there was a lady with shoulder-length hair, wearing a white tunic outfit. I noticed all of us were wearing white gowns. Then I looked to my left and saw a tall angel standing by the door. He was about twelve feet tall and looked super serious.

"As I looked forward, I saw a whiteboard and a door that looked like a back entrance reserved for VIP's. The door flung open and the teacher entered the classroom along with another tall angel. It appeared like the angel could be the teacher's assistant.

"It was quite obvious the teacher was happy, excited, and full of joy. Immediately, I recognized him as King David. He said, 'Today I am going to teach you on the subject of courage' and as he said the word *courage*, he wrote it in purple on the whiteboard. He went on to say, 'In heaven we have tests, but you are going to enjoy them. And you will want to have tests because you want to learn.' And I did enjoy them!

"The angel handed me some books as he passed out the test. The test was about seven or eight pages long and all the questions were multiple choice. I don't remember any of the questions but thank God they were multiple choice! After the class was over, King David again said, 'There is a test coming!'

"As I was leaving the class, the stern-looking angel grabbed my arm and handed me something that I had never seen before. I can't adequately describe it to you. It looked like a pen, but it was designed very differently. King David put his arm around me and said, 'Let me tell you what that is. It's a highlighter. The books in your hands are not yours yet, but while you are here, everything you highlight will only be seen by your eyes and will all be in pure gold.'

"Highlighters that are pure gold! Isn't that amazing? Our Father is very rich. I felt such love from King David and so encouraged!

"Then I went into another class. This classroom was set up completely different than the first one. There were round tables and I didn't see an angel standing by the door. I don't know who the teacher was, but he looked very wise. He had long hair and beard and wore a flowing robe that was tailored perfectly to him. It hung barely half an inch from the floor and swayed when he walked. He carried a huge Bible in his hand that was made of wood with gold finishing.

"He said, 'We're going to learn about numbers in the Bible and today we are going to learn about the number eight.' Numbers in the Bible all have a specific meaning. I remember thinking, 'This class isn't for me, but my grandmother, Billye Brim, would love it!'

"He passed out a paper to each of us with a very large eight written on it with lines on both sides. We were supposed to identify each part of the number eight because each part carried its own meaning. All the other students were very studious and busy working on the assignment, but I was just sitting there because I didn't know what to do about the number eight.

"I raised my hand and the instructor came over to help me. He looked at me, full of joy, and smiled as he opened his Bible and began to talk to me about the number eight. Suddenly I was back in my body on my couch.

"I don't remember what he said but I felt encouragement! I received a download of courage! I was a new man."

Although Branden's visitation (or vision of heaven) had much personal significance to him, I thought it very interesting that teaching in a classroom setting was included in his vision. I have heard many accounts and read many books about people who have had visions of heaven. I cannot account for all their accuracy, but one thing that I have noticed they have in common is that there is teaching and instruction that continues in heaven. It appears that knowledge will be forever increasing, and we will be forever learning.

Charles Litterer

Charles Litterer is my wife's grandfather. He served in World War I and in World War II. After the war, he worked with IBM and NASA. He was a genius with an extremely high IQ. I remember him taking me on a tour of one of his NASA projects. He helped design the wiring on the Apollo 8 spacecraft.

I'll never forget him standing outside the capsule trying to explain to me in a language I could understand what some of the wires did. As he stood there giving me information beyond my comprehension, I remember how he looked in his short-sleeve white dress shirt with a pocket protector and thin black tie. But what always impressed me was his character, integrity, and respect for authority. He was the soldier and employee that would never question his orders but would comply with a smile. It was a joy knowing him.

Several years ago, when he was late in years, he passed away to his heavenly home. My wife received a call from the nurse who was with him when he died. She told her that just before he passed into glory, he sat up straight in bed, and with a smile on his face, gave a military salute. Then he laid back down and exited this earth.

Knowing his personality and his respect for authority, I believe he saw his "Commander In Chief" and was escorted off the battlefield. I believe that just like Stephen saw into heaven before his death, many times the cord to the curtain is pulled and there is vision into the unseen realm.

Moses—Old Testament Example

On the day of His resurrection, Jesus entered the Holy of Holies in heaven to place His blood on the altar. The Bible says in Hebrews 9:24 that He entered the original Holy of Holies that was not constructed with human hands, but by the Word of God.

The heavenly Holy of Holies contained the original ark of the covenant. It was not the ark in the tabernacle or the holy temple on earth, and it was not the one that the Hebrews carried with them into battle. It was the original in heaven, not made with human hands, and never before sprinkled with blood. Jesus created this holy altar Himself to receive His own blood.

This brings up an interesting question. If the ark of the covenant and the Holy of Holies that were in Israel were constructed by the instructions of Moses, and they were copies of the originals in heaven, how did Moses know how to construct them? The answer is quite simple: Moses, like Paul the Apostle, either had a vision or a visitation to heaven himself.

Hebrews 8:5 says that Moses was told to make all things concerning the tabernacle according to the pattern that was shown to him when he was on the mountain for forty days receiving the commandments from God. The Bible tells us that everything that is seen was created from things that were not seen (Hebrews 11:3).

How long was this vision or this trip by Moses? We are not told, but we do know that it was long enough that he had time to receive lengthy instructions and measurements. When he came down from the mountain, his face was glowing so radiantly that he had to wear a veil (Exodus 34:29-35). He had been in the presence of God Almighty. Moses truly had a heavenly experience!

Moses, Stephen, Paul, and John the Apostle were mere men and they, along with countless others, have had heavenly visions and visits. As Christians, we must see historical events and biblical stories as real events and not just legends. We must realize that they were actual events that happened to people who had faith in God. The Bible teaches us that everything we receive from God, we receive by faith. You have the same faith available to you that they had. Believe and receive!

Chapter Twelve

THE MUSIC OF HEAVEN

Praise Him with the sound of the trumpet; praise Him with the lute and harp! Praise Him with the timbrel and dance; praise Him with stringed instruments and flutes! Praise Him with loud cymbals; praise Him with clashing cymbals!

PSALM 150:3-5

In the beginning God created the heavens and filled them with music. God enjoys music! The earliest mention of music took place in the heavens and its focus was on the worship of God. In those early days of creation, the morning stars (angels) sang together. God created a "worship leader" named Lucifer, the bearer of light, and this cherub led the angelic beings in the worship of Almighty God.

Lucifer was created perfect in every way, and for an unknown period of time before his rebellion against God, he led the angels of heaven in worship. Our earthly imagination cannot come close to the reality of the magnificence of pure heavenly worship. Morning stars is a symbolic term that refers to angels. Job 38:7 describes how the morning stars sang together, and all the sons of God shouted for joy.

Lucifer was created with timbrels and pipes (Ezekiel 28:13). Timbrels are tambourines and pipes are wind instruments. He was created perfect, and all that was within him was perfect. He was created for the purpose of worshiping God and he was the cherub that covers (Ezekiel 28:14). But when he sinned, God cast him out of the mountain of God declaring him profane (Ezekiel 28:15-16). He was cast to the earth (Revelation 12:9; Luke 10:18).

When Lucifer was cast down, his music was cast down with him. He retained his talent but lost his position. "Your pomp is brought down to Sheol, and the sound of your stringed instruments" (Isaiah 14:11).

The Power of Music

Music has the power to inspire and lift up, but it also has the power to destroy. Music from God can lift a person out of depression and bring peace. As we will show later, the musical notes themselves can speak to the spirit. Instrumental music without words can penetrate the spirit, but music with words touches the spirit and soul and can be used not only to inspire, but to teach and bring revelation.

In a quiet moment, have you ever had a song pop into your consciousness and, without planning it, you continue to hear the melodies and words of this song in your head? You ask yourself where the song came from. Why are you hearing this song at this time? It is often a song that was playing in the background at a store where you were shopping, or in the background of an office where you patiently sat in the waiting room. But it is usually a song you have recently heard somewhere.

This by itself proves that music is powerful and that words with a melody will be remembered much easier than words without a melody. This is why we use a song to teach our children the alphabet. We all remember the musical jingles from commercials on television, even commercials from decades ago when we were young. This brings us to this conclusion: music with words creates a deeper memory than words alone. The words to a worship song are extremely important and they connect to the heart. Here's some advice for Christian worship leaders: if we wouldn't preach it, we shouldn't sing it.

We must never forget that the enemy we are facing in our lives today is Satan and his rebellious band of fallen angels. They seek to steal, kill, and destroy the lives of mankind any way they can (John 10:10). Because music was the focus of his created being, it is the thing that he is most skilled in.

The music we listen to and the songs we sing are extremely important because they contain words, and life and death are in the power of the tongue. Studies have shown that certain types of music, when played in certain atmospheres, can help promote drug use and suicide.

God is not the author of confusion, but of peace (1 Corinthians 14:33). Music from God will never be distorted or demonic in nature, but will always be positive and uplifting. Every good and perfect gift comes from above (James 1:17). Music is a gift.

Parents have authority over their children and the God-given responsibility to protect and guide them. Children should never be allowed to privately listen to music without the parents approving it. In our current society, with the abundance of personal music devices, it is imperative that parents guard the minds of their children. Never forget that Satan is a deceiver and the nature of deception is to think what is right is wrong and wrong is right.

The original intent of music was for the purpose of worshiping God. But after Eve was deceived in the garden and Adam sinned, the door was opened for the perversion of everything on earth. When man separated himself from God, he progressively discovered the power and the influence of music. Man, who was not designed to die, began to experience death.

The animal kingdom and plant life all fell to the curse upon the earth because of the sin of man (Romans 8:20-22). Lucifer and his fallen angels began to weave perversion into music.

Through the cunningness of the fallen one, fleshly desires and pride were brought into the holy creation of music. Instead of using music to bring glorious worship and praise to God, Satan perverted it and diverted it to the worship of false gods.

Historical records of the early Babylonian civilizations tell of how they sang, danced, and clapped as they played their musical instruments to their pagan gods as well as their worship of creation (rather than the Creator). This is exactly what is taking place today. Music is spiritual and originally comes from heaven, but many heavenly melodies have been perverted with discord or with ungodly lyrics. In other words, music and lyrics that were originally created for the purpose of giving praise to God were exchanged for words of perversion. "Therefore, God also gave them up to uncleanness, in the lusts of their hearts, to dishonor their bodies among themselves, who exchanged the truth of God for the lie, and worshiped and served the creature rather than the Creator" (Romans 1:24-25).

Don't take this the wrong way. I am *not* saying that all secular music is bad, but what I am saying is we must be very watchful about what we sing and what we listen to. The truth is that music penetrates the heart and can change it. "Keep your heart with all diligence, for out of it spring the issues of life" (Proverbs 4:23).

So, how do we know if a song is an acceptable song of worship? How can we determine if music is from God and not perverted music? As a Christian, you have the Holy Spirit living inside of you and He will guide you into all truth (John 16:13). Whether music from God is loud or soft, fast or slow is irrelevant, but one thing is consistent. Music from God will always bring peace, joy, and deliverance.

Music in the Hebrew Language

The Hebrew language is unique. It has qualities and dimensions like no other language on earth. The Hebrew language is not just a method of verbal and written communication, it actually has mathematics and music encoded within it. Many ancient sages and Jewish rabbis believe that every letter of the Hebrew language has seventy dimensions, and one of its primary dimensions is music.

A Hebrew professor at a state university started a project of researching the frequencies or notes associated with each Hebrew letter. There are twenty-two letters in the Hebrew alphabet which would cover three octaves. There were also twenty-two strings on King David's harp, and each string represented a Hebrew letter. The professor fed the Hebrew letters into a computer in the order that they appear in the Psalms and beautiful music was the result.

King David was not only the king, but he was also a skilled musician. Before he was king, he played his harp for King Saul when he was tormented by demons. As he played, the demons left him, and his sound mind returned (1 Samuel 16:14-23).

Why did the demons leave? I believe when David played the notes, each vibration or frequency in the air represented a Hebrew letter. It was not just a melody that he was playing, he was literally playing words that contained the power to repel evil spirits. This is the power that true music from God contains.

Music in the Old Testament

The first mention in the Bible of people singing vocally is when the Hebrews were miraculously delivered from the Egyptians by the parting of the sea and the drowning of the enemy. When they reached the other side, it's recorded in Exodus 15:1 that Moses and all the children of Israel sang a song unto the LORD, saying, "I will sing unto the LORD, for He has triumphed gloriously! The horse and the rider He has thrown into the sea!"

King David is credited with establishing the first Israelite orchestra and choir. The purpose of this group of singers and musicians was to enhance the spiritual mood during sacred events. These musicians and singers came from the priestly tribe of Levi. In 1 Chronicles 15, King David told the leaders of the Levites to appoint their brothers as singers and to sing joyful songs accompanied by musical instruments. Then he listed the instruments he wanted used. He said they were to play lyres, harps and cymbals and they were to play these instruments joyfully making their voices heard.

Then David spoke to the leaders of the Levites to appoint their brethren to be the singers accompanied by instruments of music, stringed instruments, harps, and cymbals, by raising the voice with resounding joy.

1 CHRONICLES 15:16

King David had 288 trained members in his choir (1 Chronicles 25:7) and his choir continued under Solomon, Jehoshaphat, Josiah, Hezekiah, Ezra, and Nehemiah.

King Solomon was a songwriter who composed 1,005 songs (1 Kings 4:32). In Ecclesiastes 2:8 he said, "I also gathered for myself silver and gold and the special treasures of kings and of the provinces. I acquired male and female singers, the delights of the sons of men, and musical instruments of all kinds." In 2 Chronicles 30:21 we are told, "So the children of Israel who were present at Jerusalem kept the Feast of Unleavened Bread seven days with great gladness; and the Levites and the priests praised the LORD day by day, singing to the LORD, accompanied by loud instruments."

When the assembly of Israel presented themselves before the LORD, they were instructed to make a joyful shout unto the LORD, to serve the LORD with gladness, and to come before His presence with singing (Psalm 100:1).

During the time of Nehemiah, when the time came to dedicate the wall at Jerusalem, they sought out the Levites and took them to Jerusalem for the dedication. Nehemiah 12:27 says they did this with thanksgiving and singing, and with cymbals, stringed instruments, and harps.

The *Mishnah* (Ar. 2:6) states that in Jerusalem's second temple, "there were never fewer than twelve Levites standing on the platform as a choir, but there was no limit on the maximum number of singers."

Music from Heaven

There are numerous examples of praise and worship in the Old Testament when men would write songs of worship and sing them unto the LORD. But there is nothing that compares to heavenly songs sung by heavenly beings.

The only biblical account of angels singing on the earth is at the birth of Jesus. A multitude of the heavenly host sang for the shepherds who were in the field. Luke 2:13-14 says, "And suddenly there was with the angel a multitude of the heavenly host praising God and saying: 'Glory to God in the highest, and on earth peace, goodwill toward men!'"

This one account shows how heaven responded to the greatest miracle in history—the birth of the Son of God as a man.

When Jesus was born of a virgin for the purpose of completing the task of reconciling mankind back to God, heaven didn't respond with an earth-shattering, cataclysmic event, but rather with a heavenly choir coming to earth and singing, "Glory to God in the highest!"

It seems quite clear to me that music has always been extremely important to God, because from the very beginning, He created a worship leader in heaven to lead the angels in song. Even though the worship leader (Lucifer) rebelled, God still considered worship through music extremely important. So important in fact, that at the birth of His only begotten Son, angels were dispatched to proclaim His birth to the earth through praise and worship.

At the last supper, one of the last things that Jesus and His disciples did before His arrest and crucifixion was to sing a hymn (Matthew 26:30). At the beginning of His earthly ministry and at the end of His earthly ministry, there was music.

Harmonizing with Angels

There was a time when my home was about thirty miles from my office. On one particular evening while driving home, I began to sing a worship song. The radio was not playing, and the only thing that could be heard in my car was my own voice singing, "I love You, Lord, and I lift my voice..." After a few minutes, I could hear another voice inside the car singing with me. It was not the sound of the road, it was not the hum of the tires or the engine, it was a crystal-clear voice singing perfect harmony along with me. Although I knew I was in the vehicle by myself, I resisted the urge to look at the seat next to me and I continued to sing. The beautiful voice in the car continued to sing along with me, harmonizing perfectly.

I could feel the presence of the Lord and I had never experienced anything like that before while singing. After about ten minutes, I needed to turn onto a different highway. When I slowed down to turn, I glanced into the seat next to me and it was completely empty. No one was there, and the singing stopped. The singing may have continued in the realm of the spirit, but I could no longer hear the voice. I am convinced that when we sing unto the Lord with a pure heart, there are accompanying angelic voices that we may or may not be hearing.

A New Covenant—A New Song

Oh, sing to the LORD a new song! Sing to the LORD, all the earth.

PSALM 96:1

When Jesus put His blood on the altar in heaven, everything changed. All those who loved God and worshiped Him under the Old Covenant did so by choice. They were led by the Spirit as they wrote spiritual songs and, of course, God was very pleased with that. However, under the New Covenant, old things have passed away and all things have become new.

Those who have accepted Jesus as their Lord and Savior literally have the Holy Spirit living inside of them (Romans 8:11). The One who created Lucifer as the perfect worship leader of heaven, the One whom the angels in heaven sang to, and the One who deserves all our praise lives within us.

In Old Testament times, the Holy Spirit came upon prophets, priests, and kings for a period of time, but would then depart. There are also cases where people were filled with the Holy Spirit under the Old Covenant, but then it was temporary. They had a visitation of the Holy Spirit. But as believers under the New Covenant, the Holy Spirit lives within us. Instead of a visitation, we have a habitation.

> *Do you not know that you are the temple of God and that the Spirit of God dwells in you?*
>
> 1 CORINTHIANS 3:16

When it comes to music from heaven, what does that mean to us? New Testament believers should be able to worship in the spirit on a level that the world is not familiar with. Paul the Apostle instructed the Church at Corinth that when they prayed and sang, they should pray in the understanding and pray in the spirit, but he also told them to sing in the understanding and to sing in the spirit. In 1 Corinthians 13 Paul said, "I speak with the tongues of men and angels." But what did he mean by this? He was talking about a heavenly language that we cannot only speak in, but that we can sing in as well.

> *I will pray with the spirit, and I will also pray with the understanding. I will sing with the spirit, and I will also sing with the understanding.*
>
> 1 CORINTHIANS 14:15

Paul and Silas Delivered Through Worship

But at midnight Paul and Silas were praying and singing hymns to God, and the prisoners were listening to them.

Acts 16:25

Because we can now sing in the spirit, we can add heavenly power to our earthly praise. That's exactly what happened when Paul and Silas were in prison. When they were in Phillippi, they encountered a slave girl who was possessed by a demonic spirit. She was demonically gifted in the area of fortune telling.

For some time, she followed Paul and Silas proclaiming, "These men are the servants of the Most High God, who proclaim to us the way of salvation" (Acts 16:17). But after several days, Paul became greatly annoyed by this, and turning to her, he spoke to the spirit that possessed her saying, "I command you in the name of Jesus Christ to come out of her." And the spirit came out of her that very hour" (Acts 16:18).

This girl was working for men who had been making great profit from her divination. But after the spirit departed and her fortune telling ceased, her masters realized that their method of making profit was now gone. So, they dragged Paul and Silas to the authorities where they were beaten with rods then thrown into prison.

Because the jailor had been given a specific command, he put them in the inner prison, and he locked their feet in stocks.

He wanted to make sure they were secure, because the rule of that day was that if a prisoner escaped, the one guarding him would himself receive their punishment.

The Roman prisons in Paul's day were extremely inhumane. They were rat-infested and there were no toilet facilities. Beaten prisoners with open wounds would lie in sewage. Long-term prisoners would almost certainly die from disease, infection, or starvation. So, there they were, Paul and Silas, beaten with rods, open wounds, and their feet fastened in stocks so that they had very little movement. It was midnight and at sunrise more torture awaited them.

But instead of complaining about their dire circumstances, they believed God would deliver them. Like Daniel in the lion's den, they trusted God. So, at midnight they sang hymns to God. And suddenly there was a great earthquake. The foundations of the prison were shaken and all the doors were opened. Everyone who was bound with chains was released. As a final result, the keeper of the prison and his entire family were saved (Acts 16:25-33).

You may be going through a time where you feel trapped. You may think there's no way out, but I encourage you to do what Paul and Silas did. Midnight was the darkest time for them. At your "darkest hour," instead of complaining and focusing on the problem, pray and sing to the Problem Solver. This is the key to having your chains drop off, bringing you freedom.

Singing and Making Melody

Speaking to one another in psalms and hymns and spiritual songs, singing and making melody in your heart to the Lord.

EPHESIANS 5:19

As Christians under the New Covenant, we are told to speak to one another in psalms and hymns and spiritual songs, singing and making melody in our hearts to the Lord. We are clearly told to express ourselves with spiritual melodies. God's will is expressed in His Word and His Word shows His desire for spiritual music.

In Paul's letter to the Colossians, he admonished the Church to let the word of Christ dwell in them with wisdom, and to teach and admonish one another in psalms, hymns, and spiritual songs so that they could sing with grace in their hearts (Colossians 3:16). A part of the ministry of the New Testament Church is to minister to each other by song. Sadly, this personal music ministry has been partially ignored throughout much of the modern Church.

It has always saddened me when people arrive late for church and drift into the auditorium near the end of the music portion of the service. Others will stand and talk in the entry hall until the music and singing has concluded. I understand if a person is working in the service in the ministry of helps or in leadership that there may be other duties that need to be attended to. Likewise, the person who will be delivering the message from the Word may be seeking God and not yet in the auditorium. However, this cannot be an excuse to avoid precious time of worship with spiritual singing.

While at a ministers' conference several years ago, a pastor told me that at times he wished he didn't have a worship team, although they were actually quite necessary. He went on to say that the worship team's purpose was like a call to worship that allowed people to finish their conversations and their coffee before coming into the auditorium for the true "meat" of the service. How sad that this minister didn't understand the ministry of musical worship directed by the Spirit of God.

There is a definite connection between heaven and earth when a born-again believer sings in the spirit. The actual phrase "singing in the spirit" implies that a person who is in the physical realm is connecting with the Lord of the spiritual realm and through this connection, God speaks to us. When we open our hearts to heavenly, spiritual music, we become candidates to hear a heavenly word from God.

Music in the Ages to Come

After the rapture of the Church there is a time period of seven years before the return of Jesus to the earth (the Second Coming), when He sets up His kingdom for His one-thousand-year reign. During this seven-year period while the enemy is attempting to destroy mankind and possess the earthly Jerusalem, the saints are having a glorious time in heaven where they are experiencing the judgment seat of Christ and the marriage supper of the Lamb.

While God's wrath is being poured out upon the earth, the Apostle John (in his Revelation of Jesus Christ and future events) described how the four living creatures and the twenty-four elders fell down before the Lamb, each having a harp and golden bowls of incense, which are the prayers of the saints. And they sang a new song, saying (Revelation 5:8-9):

> *You are worthy to take the scroll,*
> *And to open its seals;*
> *For You were slain,*
> *And have redeemed us to God by Your blood*
> *Out of every tribe and tongue and people and nation,*
> *And have made us kings and priests to our God;*
> *And we shall reign on the earth.*
>
> REVELATION 5:10

Later in his vision, John heard a voice from heaven that sounded like the voice of many waters and like loud thunder. Then he heard the sound of harpists playing their harps and they sang a new song before the throne and before the four living creatures and the elders. No one could learn the song except the 144,000 who were redeemed from the earth (Revelation 14:2-3).

Then John saw another sign in heaven. He saw seven angels having the last seven plagues and he saw something like a sea of glass mingled with fire. And he saw those who overcame the beast, his image, and his mark standing on the sea of glass. They all had harps of God and sang the song of Moses and the song of the Lamb, saying:

> *Great and marvelous are Your works,*
> *Lord God Almighty!*
> *Just and true are Your ways,*
> *O King of the saints!*
> *Who shall not fear You, O Lord, and glorify Your*
> *name?*
> *For You alone are holy.*
> *For all nations shall come and worship before You,*
> *For Your judgments have been manifested.*
>
> REVELATION 15:3-4

There are numerous references throughout the Bible about music in heaven and on earth, but we can never forget this: God is the originator and creator of music. He created it as a method for all creatures, whether in heaven or on earth, to worship Him. And ultimately, all creation will sing unto the Lord.

> *All the earth shall worship You and sing praises to You;*
> *they shall sing praises to Your name.*
>
> PSALM 66:4

Chapter Thirteen

LIFE DURING THE MILLENNIUM

And on the seventh day God ended His work which
He had done, and He rested on the seventh day from
all His work which He had done. Then God blessed the
seventh day and sanctified it, because in it He rested
from all His work which God had created and made.

GENESIS 2:2-3

When Jesus returns to defeat the evil of the Great Tribulation at the Second Coming, He will set up His millennial kingdom here on the earth. Some may wonder why we would need to understand the millennial rule of Christ on the earth as we are detailing the journey of a Christian to eternity. The answer is simply this: The Church will be ruling and reigning with Christ throughout the millennium. Before we move into our eternal dwelling in the New Jerusalem, we must travel through this time period.

Although the Church will be based in the heavenly Jerusalem during the millennium, we will be ruling and reigning with the Lord Jesus over the entire earth (Revelation 20:4). This implies that there will be much interaction with the earthly population who will continue to live their lives in flesh-and-blood human bodies.

> *And they sang a new song, saying: "You are worthy to take the scroll, and to open its seals; for You were slain, and have redeemed us to God by Your blood out of every tribe and tongue and people and nation, and have made us kings and priests to our God; and we shall reign on the earth."*
>
> REVELATION 5:9-10

There are several references to the "day of the Lord" in the Bible. Some of these references are referring directly to the one thousand years that Jesus rules and reigns over the entire earth. Remember that one day with the Lord is as a thousand years, and a thousand years is as a day (2 Peter 3:8). The final day of the Lord is the millennium.

The millennial reign of Christ begins after Jesus returns to the earth with the saints of God and His angels to defeat the powers that are attempting to conquer Jerusalem at the end of the seven-year Great Tribulation. This is when the beast and the false prophet are cast alive into the lake of fire

(Revelation 19:20) and Satan is bound in the bottomless pit for one thousand years.

> *Then I saw an angel coming down from heaven, having the key to the bottomless pit and a great chain in his hand. He laid hold of the dragon, that serpent of old, who is the Devil and Satan, and bound him for a thousand years; and he cast him into the bottomless pit, and shut him up, and set a seal on him, so that he should deceive the nations no more till the thousand years were finished. But after these things he must be released for a little while.*
> REVELATION 20:1-3

The Sheep and Goat Judgment

After Jesus has reclaimed the world as His own and as He sets up His kingdom to rule and reign for one thousand years, the decision must be made on who will be allowed to populate the earth in the millennial kingdom. It is at this time that He will judge nations and individuals to determine who is worthy to live under His rule.

Jesus said that when He returns, He will sit on the throne of His glory. All the nations of the earth will stand before Him, and He will separate the people as a shepherd divides his sheep. This judgment of the Gentile tribulation survivors will be the judgment of the nations.

*When the Son of Man comes in His glory, and all the
holy angels with Him, then He will sit on the throne of
His glory. All the nations will be gathered before Him,
and He will separate them one from another, as a shepherd divides his sheep from the goats. And He will set
the sheep on His right hand, but the goats on the left.*
Matthew 25:31-33

All of those who are left alive on the earth and who have
survived the Great Tribulation will be divided into two groups—
the sheep and the goats. He will separate the surviving believers
(sheep) from the surviving unbelievers (goats).

Sheep

Immediately after the rapture, the total population of the
earth will be the unbelievers who are left behind. During the
Great Tribulation, some of these unbelievers will receive Jesus
as their Messiah and will not take the mark of the beast. This
group of people were unbelievers before the rapture and, of
course, were not caught up with the Church. They remained
on the earth in human bodies and received Jesus as the Messiah
sometime during the seven-year Great Tribulation. They are
"tribulation saints."

Some of these tribulation saints will be martyred, but at
the Second Coming of Jesus, those martyred will be resurrected into natural human bodies and they, along with those
who were not martyred for their faith but endured to the end,

will be counted as "sheep." They will enter the millennium to populate the kingdom of God on earth.

> *But he who endures to the end shall be saved.*
>
> Matthew 24:13

This group is not to be confused with the Church. Remember, the Church received glorified bodies at the rapture and was united with Jesus at the marriage supper of the Lamb. At the rapture, the Church became a closed group. The age of grace is over, the marriage of the Lamb is over, and they are sealed as trophies of His grace for all eternity.

The tribulation survivors who are sorted as sheep will enter the millennium in their natural bodies with physical, mental, and spiritual imperfections that include a sin nature. Millennial life for the Gentile will be much the same as life today. But in order to have healing, honoring Israel is essential. The tree of life holds healings in its leaves and can only be accessed by those who bless Israel.

Goats

At the sheep and goat judgment, the unbelievers (goats) who took the mark of the beast or did not receive Jesus as the Messiah will be cast into the everlasting fire.

> *Then He will also say to those on the left hand, "Depart from Me, you cursed, into the everlasting fire prepared for the devil and his angels."*
>
> Matthew 25:41

Likewise, the nations will be judged as nations. The nations that do not bless Israel will be considered "goat nations" and will not exist as a national state during the millennium.

National Israel

While the Gentile believers will populate the nations, the Jewish believers will live in Israel. The natural Jews (the descendants of Abraham, Isaac, and Jacob) who survived the tribulation and received Jesus as the Messiah will continue into the millennial kingdom in their natural human bodies in the national state of Israel on earth. Likewise, all the faithful Jews of centuries past will also be resurrected into natural bodies and will also occupy national Israel throughout the millennium (Daniel 12:1-2).

Life in Israel will continue with temple rituals that the Jews will be required to practice. Because they are in mortal bodies, they will still be subject to sin. Daily sacrifices for their sin will serve as a continual reminder of how the Lord Jesus died for them (Ezekiel 40-46). Israel will be at peace and the wealth of the nations will be given to Israel (Isaiah 66:12). Throughout the millennium, Israel will remain faithful to the Lord Jesus.

At the Second Coming, there will be an earthquake, and as a result, there will be great geological changes in the Middle East (Zechariah 14:4). As Israel moves into the millennial kingdom, its borders will be restored very closely to the borders told to Moses in Numbers 34. The western border will be the Mediterranean Sea. The eastern border will be from Kadesh-Barnea via Zin and the Salt Sea to Zedad and Hamath in the north. The southern border will range from Kadesh-Barnea to the Brook of Egypt and the northern border from the Mediterranean Sea to Hamath to Zedad. The borders described in Ezekiel 47 are very similar to those described in Numbers 34 with minor exceptions.

Life on Earth

"It shall come to pass that before they call, I will answer; and while they are still speaking, I will hear. The wolf and the lamb shall feed together, the lion shall eat straw like the ox, and dust shall be the serpent's food. They shall not hurt nor destroy in all My holy mountain," says the LORD.

ISAIAH 65:24-25

During the millennium, the earth will be restored to its pre-flood grandeur. It will be an amazing place to live! There will be peace and plenty like never seen before. The people who have survived the Great Tribulation will stand in awe of the magnificence of the earthly kingdom under the rule of the Lord Jesus and His saints. The atmosphere will be pure, and the earth will be uncontaminated. The poisonous reptiles and carnivorous beasts will cease to be a threat. The lamb will lay down with the lion. Human life expectancy will increase (Isaiah 65:20), and those who have just survived the previous seven years of the worst time in human history will be blessed beyond measure!

> *Now it shall come to pass in the latter days that the mountain of the LORD's house shall be established on the top of the mountains and shall be exalted above the hills; and all nations shall flow to it. Many people shall come and say, "Come, and let us go up to the mountain of the LORD, to the house of the God of Jacob; He will teach us His ways, and we shall walk in His paths."*
>
> *For out of Zion shall go forth the law, and the word of the LORD from Jerusalem.*
>
> *He shall judge between the nations and rebuke many people; they shall beat their swords into plowshares, and their spears into pruning hooks; nation shall not lift up sword against nation, neither shall they learn war anymore.*
>
> ISAIAH 2:2-4

After Adam and Eve were expelled from the garden, it took 1,656 years for pre-flood mankind to deteriorate into a level of sin that brought God's judgment upon the earth. During this time, longevity was so long that there were multiple generations of elders who retained memories of earth's early days. But as time passed, the memory of the perfection in the garden was lost and the sin nature of man became more prevalent.

Likewise, those living in the millennium in natural bodies on the earth will not have born-again spirits, and thus, will continue to have the sin nature of natural man. They will live under the law and not grace. As time passes, the memory of their deliverance from the Great Tribulation will fade and some will desire to rebel against the godly kingdom.

The Gentile nations will need to be represented each year when Israel celebrates the Feast of Tabernacles. Failure to attend will bring strict punishment. The twenty-ninth chapter of Ezekiel is the prophecy of Egypt's failure to comply. The result is a forty-year period when Egypt becomes completely desolate with its population being dispersed into the other nations of the world. Then at the end of the forty years, the Lord brings the citizens of Egypt home. This prophecy will be fulfilled during the millennium and is an example of how the judgment of the Lord will be implemented.

> *And it shall come to pass that everyone who is left of all the nations which came against Jerusalem shall go up from year to year to worship the King, the LORD of hosts, and to keep the Feast of Tabernacles. And it shall be that whichever of the families of the earth do not come up to Jerusalem to worship the King, the LORD of hosts, on them there will be no rain.*
>
> *If the family of Egypt will not come up and enter in, they shall have no rain; they shall receive the plague with which the LORD strikes the nations who do not come up to keep the Feast of Tabernacles. This shall be the punishment of Egypt and the punishment of all*

the nations that do not come up to keep the Feast of Tabernacles.

In that day "HOLINESS TO THE LORD" shall be engraved on the bells of the horses. The pots in the LORD's house shall be like the bowls before the altar.

ZECHARIAH 14:16-20

The Coming Rebellion

God has always been just. He has always given His creation a choice. We know that He has placed before us life and death, then to make sure we understand, He tells us to choose life (Deuteronomy 30:19). Why would He have to tell us to choose life? It is because man, without being born again into the Church, has a sin nature that was inherited from the fall of man in the garden. By one man (Adam) sin was brought into the world and by one man (Jesus) sin was taken out for those who believed during the age of grace (Romans 5:12-13). That group (the Church) will be taken out of the earth at the rapture, and those who are left will still have the sin nature of Adam and will return to the law.

Living in natural, flesh-and-blood bodies, the population on the earth during the millennium will continue to bear children (Isaiah 65:23). The children born in this dispensation must make their own choice. They must decide whether to accept Jesus as the Messiah, their Lord and Ruler, or reject Him. For those born during the millennium, no one can make this choice for them. Like everyone of past generations, they must choose for themselves.

As decades and centuries pass, the memories of the Great Tribulation judgments will fade. In each generation there will be a number of those who reject the Lord. Their obedience to His rule will only be given reluctantly and with growing resentment. When Satan is released from the pit at the end of the one thousand years, he will easily gather these subculture rebels, and through his deception, they will follow him to their own destruction.

Because Jesus will rule as a righteous king with a fist of iron (Revelation 2:27), He will not allow any perversion under His rule. But the human nature of some will rise up, becoming resentful. These are like the ones living on the earth right now that Satan uses to do his work.

The Final Judgment of Evil

The blessing of the Lord is always received with great joy. When God supernaturally, through His mercy, delivers us from destruction (Psalm 34:19) and blesses us with peace we do not deserve, we are always thankful. However, throughout history, it has been proven that in extended times of great blessing, man begins to take the blessing for granted with the memory of past peril being forgotten. Sadly, this condition is repeated one last time during the millennium.

As we said earlier, the generations will gradually forget the tribulation as time passes and begin to feel entitled to their blessings and disgruntled with authority. This underlying contempt for authority will cause mankind to become easy prey to the deception of Satan after he is released at the end of the millennium. It appears that the rebellion will only happen among the Gentile nations, because there is no mention in the Bible of Israel falling away during the millennium.

Despite the rule of the righteous King, the deception of Satan will spread throughout the earth into the Gentile nations. As the millennium draws to a close, those who hate righteousness and who have developed an underground culture of sin and rebellion will be gathered by Satan when he is released from the bottomless pit.

Gathering an army that the Bible describes as more numerous than the sand of the sea (Revelation 20:8), they will surround the camp of the saints in the beloved city of Jerusalem. In his foolishness, Satan will once again think that he can overpower God's kingdom. In a final strike of vengeance, God will send fire out of heaven to devour Satan and his entire army. All the planning, all of the work, and all of the desire of Satan is destroyed in one half of one verse in the Bible!

> *They went up on the breadth of the earth and surrounded the camp of the saints and the beloved city.*

And fire came down from God out of heaven and devoured them.

REVELATION 20:9

Then the great deceiver, the devil, the anointed cherub who was in heaven (named Lucifer who became Satan) will join the beast and the false prophet in the lake of fire and brimstone. Then the execution of his sentence will be complete. They will be tormented day and night throughout eternity. It will be the ultimate punishment for the greatest evil being that has ever existed, Satan.

The devil, who deceived them, was cast into the lake of fire and brimstone where the beast and the false prophet are. And they will be tormented day and night forever and ever.

REVELATION 20:10

It is interesting that in the sentencing of Satan, the false prophet, and the beast we discover a truth—there will be day and night forever.

The Final Judgment of Man

After Satan has been removed from the earth, there is a judgment called the great white throne judgment. At this judgment the King of Kings and Lord of Lords will sit upon a great white throne. The graves will be opened and all the unrighteous people who previously died on the earth and were not resurrected at the rapture or at the Second Coming, will be res-urrected at this time. The sea will give up the dead within it, and Death and Hades will give up the dead who are in them (Revelation 20:13). And Death and Hades will then be cast into the lake of fire.

At the great white throne judgment, everyone will be judged by their works, which will not meet the standard of righteous-ness. Because man will be judged by his own works, all sin will be exposed and the price of sin, without the blood of Jesus, is death. Each one will be judged individually and as the Book of Life is opened, anyone not found to be written in the Book of Life will be cast into the lake of fire, which is called the second death.

> *Then I saw a great white throne and Him who sat on it, from whose face the earth and the heaven fled away. And there was found no place for them. And I saw the dead, small and great, standing before God, and books were opened. And another book was opened, which is the Book of Life. And the dead were judged accord-ing to their works, by the things which were written in the books.*
>
> REVELATION 20:11-12

> *Then Death and Hades were cast into the lake of fire. This is the second death. And anyone not found writ-ten in the Book of Life was cast into the lake of fire.*
>
> REVELATION 20:14-15

The Good News

The good news for the Church is simply this: We will be ruling and reigning in glorified bodies throughout the millennium with our home base in the heavenly Jerusalem. We will not be exposed to the underlying corruption developing on the earth that will end with the Gog and Magog war, and the final destruction of evil.

In the Apostle John's vision of future events, after the great white throne judgment, he saw a new heaven and a new earth. Then he saw the New Jerusalem descending out of heaven prepared as a bride adorned for her husband (Revelation 21:2). A city is known by those living in it, and the inhabitants of the New Jerusalem will be the Church, living in the place that Jesus has prepared for them, in their glorified bodies.

And a loud voice from heaven spoke, saying, "Behold, the tabernacle of God is with men, and He will dwell with them, and they shall be His people. God Himself will be with them and be their God" (Revelation 21:3).

This is the glorious moment that all the redeemed have been longing for, the moment when God will live with man and man will live with God. The Bible says at this time God will wipe away every tear from their eyes and there shall be no more death, no more sorrow, no more crying, and no more pain (Revelation 21:4). The things of the past will have passed away and a fresh start for mankind will begin as we step into eternity.

Chapter Fourteen

YOUR FINAL DESTINATION

Nevertheless we, according to His promise, look for new heavens and a new earth in which righteousness dwells.

2 PETER 3:13

God is timeless. By this we mean that He has no beginning and no end. He has always existed, and He will continue to exist, without end. When He sent Jesus to the earth as His Son in the flesh, Jesus was revealed as the only begotten Son of God throughout eternity.

When the Holy Spirit impregnated the young Jewish girl named Mary, she became the earthly mother, and the Holy Spirit became the Father of the earthly manifestation of the Son of God—Jesus. Jesus was literally the Son of the Eternal God living in a body of flesh on the earth.

And the Word became flesh and dwelt among us, and we beheld His glory, the glory as of the only begotten of the Father, full of grace and truth.

JOHN 1:14

Jesus made an astounding proclamation to His disciples. He said, "If you've seen Me, you've seen the Father" (John 14:9), "for the Father and I are One" (John 10:30). We know that the Father, the Son, and the Holy Spirit are one and are timeless.

Hebrews 13:8 says that Jesus Christ is the same yesterday, today, and forever. And in Malachi 3:6 God proclaimed this of Himself, "For I am the LORD, I do not change." Because God does not change throughout eternity, we can be assured that His promise of eternal life to us who believe will not be revoked.

All the Time in the World

It has been said that time is what keeps everything from happening at once. Time is relative, and the urgency of time is determined by the length of time that a project requires as well as by the amount of time that can be used for the project. Time has been defined as the indefinite, continued progress of existence and events divided into three categories: past, present, and future. Time can be measured in many different ways such as minutes and hours, days and years, decades and millenniums. But regardless of how it's defined, time is a steady movement forward that will forever be measured.

The same scripture that tells us that our hope of eternal life is in God and that He cannot lie, also reveals that God promised this to us before time began.

> *In hope of eternal life which God, who cannot lie, promised before time began.*
>
> Titus 1:2

Since time has a beginning, then time must have had a Creator. Almighty God, through His Word, created everything seen and unseen. Like man, time has no end and will continue throughout eternity. But God is timeless and lives on the outside of time.

How do we know that the measurement of time will continue? God commanded that Passover is to be observed forever (Exodus 12:14) and He commanded the feast of unleavened bread to likewise be observed forever (Exodus 12:17). There are more examples, but these two show that even though time will be unlimited and eternal, there will still be markers in time. Otherwise there would be no way of knowing when to observe the feasts that are to be eternal.

Another indicator in Scripture that markers in time will continue is in Revelation 22:2. It says that the leaves on the tree of life will yield its fruit monthly.

There is an old gospel song that says, "time will be no more." In one respect, that is so very true. When time is so limitless that it is called eternity, the urgency of time is eliminated.

Feeling impatient and having trouble waiting on the promises of God is a result of feeling the restriction of time. But when we step into our heavenly existence with our glorified bodies, there will no longer be any restriction of time as we now know it.

Living our daily lives with all the responsibilities that life brings can be challenging. Raising and training children while working to earn a living, keeping up with household chores, arranging transportation and meals, as well as all the other time-consuming duties of life sometimes makes us feel like throwing up our hands and saying, "I just don't have enough time to do everything that needs to be done!"

But can you imagine walking into a cluttered storage room knowing you have all the time you needed to clean it up, even if it was 250 million years? And if the job wasn't completed by then, you could get another 250 million years? Can you imagine how much less tension there would be? You would begin to realize that even though time was moving forward, the urgency of time would not exist.

On another note, can you imagine taking your sailboat down to the crystal sea to go sailing for a few thousand years (just because you want to), and when you return, you have not used up any of your time? These thoughts may seem like fiction, but with a limitless God with limitless creation abilities, with us living in glorified bodies, and with time never expiring (but continuing), there will never be anything that would take "too long" to do!

The Jewish View of Time

In the western way of thinking, time is linear. However, the ancient Hebrew concept of time is that time is circular and eventually circles back upon itself, making it never ending. In the same way that a traditional clock is not a timeline, but the hands move in a circular motion and eventually return to the same position, the ancient Hebrews of the Bible did not see time with a singularly defined beginning and end. They saw time as a continual cycle of beginnings and endings, much like a helix.

A helix is a scientific term describing a three-dimensional spiral curve. In the same way that threads on a bolt continually circle it without touching or overlapping, only moving upward, the Hebrew concept of time is also circular in nature, with a continual unending movement upward toward God.

Because the western culture sees time as linear, it's much more difficult to understand the unending concept of time. With a circular view of time, our perspective of the beginning and the end of earth and man's days on the earth changes.

The Dimension of Time

Dr. Albert Einstein had great insight in considering the nature of our physical universe. He understood that we do not live strictly in three dimensions of length, width, and height, but that time itself is a fourth physical dimension. It is this insight that led him to his famous Theory of General Relativity.

Time is now known to be a physical property, and it is said that time varies with mass, acceleration, and gravity. In God's Word He declares that He alone knows the end from the beginning. Because He is the Creator of all things in all dimensions, His perception of time is different than ours.

> *Remember the former things of old, for I am God, and there is no other; I am God, and there is none like Me, declaring the end from the beginning, and from ancient times things that are not yet done, saying, "My counsel shall stand, and I will do all My pleasure."*
>
> ISAIAH 46:9-10

Picture an automobile parked at a railroad crossing watching a train pass by. The person in the automobile is only able to see a few box cars as they pass by, and as the cars in front pass out of sight, other cars pass into view and this continues until the train has completely passed by. At the same time, someone can be observing this same train from a helicopter. Although the speed and location of the train have not changed, the person in the helicopter sees the engine and the caboose, as well as all the box cars in between, at the same time.

Although this is just an illustration, it is similar to the way God views time. Man is living day by day, watching the days pass one at a time, when God, who is the Creator of days, sees the end from the beginning from His viewpoint.

The God of creation is also the God of eternity future. Without affecting your free choice, God has seen the future and knows your choice before you make it. The glories of heaven that are described in His Word are not something that He hopes will happen, but He has seen the "end of the train" and to Him, our hope is His reality.

Back to the Future

I have always been curious about time travel. Many years ago, there was a series of movies that came out called *Back to the Future*. In these movies, a scientist discovered how he could easily move forward and backward through time.

According to many who teach modern physics, time travel is impossible. They believe that while the past can be viewed with the artifacts and images that have been left behind, to actually enter into a past existence is beyond the realm of true science. Likewise, they believe travel into the future is impossible because the future has not yet been established, nor does it currently exist.

Spiritually, this is an interesting subject to explore. When a person receives Jesus as Lord and Savior (becoming born again), the Bible says that their sins are eliminated and no longer remembered (Hebrews 8:12). How can something that existed in the past be removed from the past? While time travel is science fiction to mankind, to God it is not, because in a way that we cannot currently understand, God moves into our past and erases the existence of our sin. Under the New Covenant, our sins are not just hidden, they are eradicated! We are cleansed of all sin (1 John 1:9).

Dr. Gary Wood saw the evidence of this when he was in heaven. He saw an angel open a book that contained all the events of a person's life on earth, and with a cloth the angel wiped the pages. The writing vanished and the pages turned red, leaving only a name. When he asked what that meant, he was told, "The red represents the cleansing blood of Jesus, your Savior, and the names were transferred to the Lamb's Book of Life and the sins were remembered no more."

Saul, the Pharisee, became a Christian on the road to Damascus and his name was changed to Paul the Apostle, who wrote half of the New Testament. When he wrote of his old nature dying, he didn't say that his old man died on the road to Damascus, but rather he said his old nature was crucified with Christ (Romans 6:6). What does this mean? His old nature was crucified when Jesus died on the cross. Throughout eternity, because of God's grace, he will be treated as though his old nature never existed.

From another viewpoint, the prophecies of the Bible concerning what will happen during the tribulation, the millennium, and eternity could only be known to man by revelation from God, through the Holy Spirit. But let me ask you this question. How did God know unless He had already traveled into the future to observe what would take place?

When Moses asked God to tell him who it was that was sending him, God said tell them that "I AM" sent you. He didn't say tell them "I Was." He didn't say tell them "I Will Be." He said tell them "I AM" has sent me to you (Exodus 3:14). Within the name of God is all past, present, and future. We can be assured that throughout eternity wherever we are and wherever we go, God has already seen it and prepared it for us.

So, when will our journey begin into this wondrous future that God has already ordained? The answer is, for the Christian, we are not waiting for a future, we are already living in it. The day you received Jesus as your Lord and Savior, just like Paul the Apostle, your old nature and your sin was crucified with Christ nearly two thousand years ago. Your past has been forgiven and eradicated, and you are now in the process of moving from glory to glory (2 Corinthians 3:18).

Will We Remember the Past?

...Past troubles will be forgotten and hidden from my sight. Look! I'm creating a new heaven and a new earth: past events won't be remembered; they won't come to mind.

ISAIAH 65:16-17 (CEB)

This passage has been used by many to say that in heaven we will have no memory whatsoever of our previous lives and that our past will be completely erased from our consciousness. But that is not the case.

In context, these verses are not saying that all memory will be lost, they're simply saying that the troubling memories will no longer be troubling because the pain of the past will be eliminated. In the same way, Paul said that we should forget those things that lie behind (Philippians 3:13). We will remember things from life on earth, but without the pain because the memories of the past will be overshadowed by the joy of the present deliverance.

One of the beautiful promises in the Word of God is that Jesus has paid the price for our healing and deliverance. When we speak of healing, often people think only of their physical body being healed. But we are told that Jesus has also paid the price for our mental and emotional well-being. A person who has been abused physically, sexually, or mentally can supernaturally, by the power of God, be delivered from the trauma of the past.

Through my years in ministry, I have heard countless testimonies from people who have been abused as a child, sexually molested by a relative, or verbally assaulted to the extent that it took away their self-esteem. And many of these people, by the power and grace of God, were delivered so that their past no longer affected the future. Their hearts were clean, they had forgiven the abuser and they moved on living their life with great joy. It's very interesting that in each and every one of these cases they still remembered their past, but they no longer felt the pain of the past.

One woman told me that for most of her life she had lived in fear and torment because of the abuse she had experienced as a young girl. Sometimes she would wake up in the middle of the night screaming because she had a dream that her abuser had crawled into bed with her. This affected every aspect of her life. But after she had been delivered from this abuse, the dreams were gone, the torment was gone, she was happily married, sleeping well, and could now share with others how they could also be set free. She told me her husband wanted her to forget the past and she told him she had, and in a way, that was true. She could still remember the historical events of her childhood, but without the pain.

Likewise, in our eternal home we will not have our memory erased, but like the woman who was delivered, the pain and trauma of the past will be gone forever. Every tear will be wiped away, sin and death will no longer exist, and our joy will be complete (Revelation 21:4).

As a Christian, you will not exist as a different person throughout eternity, but as a born-again glorified human with gratitude and gratefulness for the salvation you have been freely given. Like a person who has been deathly ill and receives healing, the joy of the healing is amplified by the memory of the sickness. The joy of our salvation is amplified by the memory of what it was like to be lost. And our days in our new heavenly home will be amplified by the memory of what our Savior has delivered us from.

History will not be changed and our memory of our previous life and family will not be lost, but the glory of the New Jerusalem and our life with the Lord will by far overshadow the past.

Eternity is Limitless

The galaxies, stars, planets, quasars and other phenomena in space were put into place for future eternity. The limitlessness of time alone requires that creation be massive beyond comprehension, possibly even limitless.

It is not inconceivable that the limitless God of eternity created man in His image and in His likeness, not only to look like and act like Him, but to be like Him. Ephesians 5:1 tells us that we are to be imitators of God in the same way that children imitate their parents, doing what their parents do. The implication from this verse is that man is not only to look like and act like God but is to imitate Him in what He does.

Of course, man will never be God, nor should we attempt to step beyond the boundaries of our creation, but if God is a creator of things, then in the limitless eternity where time is irrelevant and space is endless, there could be a place where nothing has yet been created. Possibly in eternity, this could be a place where we will "call those things that do not exist as though they did" (Romans 4:17). While this may be considered fantasy or speculation, there's nothing scripturally that indicates otherwise. It is something to ponder.

I'm quite sure that everything that God has for us has not been written down, nor even thought of yet in the mind of man. But one thing is for sure. With limitless time, limitless resources, and limitless travel abilities we will see things we've never seen, do things we've never done, and experience things in realms and dimensions presently unknown.

Your Future is Bright

In this book, you have read what the Bible says is your future. As a born-again Christian, you will be moving from glory to glory, with each level of glory being more glorious than the preceding level. Ultimately, you will be in eternity. You will be living in a glorified body that is equal to the body of our Lord and Savior, Jesus. You will have a home in the New Jerusalem that cannot be compared in any way to any mansion on earth. The splendor and magnificence of what Jesus has prepared for you cannot be expressed in earthly words.

You will be an individual with individual desires and future dreams. You will have individuality because you will be given a name that only He knows (Revelation 2:17). You will have His name on your forehead (Revelation 22:4). He is yours and you are His. You will have creativity and you will have friendships that were developed on earth and new friendships developed in heaven. The universe and beyond will forever be yours to explore. There will never be a time of boredom or sadness. Every tear will be wiped away. Death and the fear of loss will be eliminated.

We are not told much in the Scriptures about life on earth after the millennium and into eternity, but we do know this: life on earth will continue and will be the eternal home of the righteous (Isaiah 66:21-22).

Once I heard a man comment that heaven would be a very boring place. How ridiculous! As a glorified saint, you will walk in the likeness and image of your Creator. The things that are a joy here on earth will pale by comparison to their counterpart in heaven. Your creativity, your travel, and your abilities will be so far beyond that of natural man that boredom on any level will be an absolute impossibility!

Of course, your memories will be precious, but you will develop countless new memories as the markers of time pass. Your times of worship will bring the closeness to Jesus you have always desired. You will be one with Him and He will be one with you.

Human imagination cannot even begin to grasp the infinity of God and the limitlessness of time. There will be no regret, there will be no failure, but the God of love and the God of light will fill you with a never-ending life of peace!

He who testifies to these things says, "Surely I am coming quickly." Amen. Even so, come, Lord Jesus!

REVELATION 22:20

Our best days are yet to come! Come quickly, Lord Jesus!

About Larry Ollison

Dr. Larry Ollison, B.A., M.A., Ph.D., Th.D., is founder and senior pastor of Walk on the Water Faith Church in Osage Beach, Missouri, and founder of Larry Ollison Ministries. With over fifty years in the ministry, he is a popular speaker nationally and internationally and ministers the word of faith through radio, television, internet, and daily e-mail devotionals. Dr. Ollison is the author of eight books (including *The Power of Grace, The Practical Handbook for Christian Living, Breaking the Cycle of Offense, Life is in the Blood*, and *The Paradise of God*). Dr. Ollison and his wife, Loretta, have two children and six grandchildren.

The Harrison House Vision

Proclaiming the truth and the power
of the Gospel of Jesus Christ with excellence.
Challenging Christians
to live victoriously,
grow spiritually,
know God intimately.

Connect with us on

Facebook @ HarrisonHousePublishers

and Instagram @ HarrisonHousePublishing

so you can stay up to date with news

about our books and our authors.

Visit us at **www.harrisonhouse.com**

for a complete product listing as well as

monthly specials for wholesale distribution.